T0334272

'This book tells stories of teacher learning that all language professionals can benefit from. The experience of novice teachers in Malaysia reflects practice in many contexts, and teachers, mentors, teacher educators and researchers will gain fresh perspectives and novel insights from these accounts of mentored learning'.

– Dr Richard Kiely, University of Southampton, UK

Professional Development through Mentoring

In their book, Othman and Senom provide a unique insight into the challenges faced by novice English as a Second Language (ESL) teachers and establish how mentoring can provide effective support for new teachers' professional development. The book demonstrates the theoretical background for viewing mentoring as a process crucial to novice teachers' development, particularly to the teachers' ability to succeed and grow in a specific workplace environment. Using case studies from a Malaysian context, this book provides a comprehensive understanding of how mentoring can serve as a strategy to facilitate the transition of novice ESL teachers from a teacher education programme to life in real classrooms. Through its case studies, the book will examine both theoretical and practical issues for mentors, teacher educators, policymakers, and administrators when mentoring new ESL teachers. This book will be valuable to researchers who are particularly interested in exploring novice teachers' identity development, and experienced teachers to help guide new teachers through the socialization process in their schools.

Juliana Othman, Ph.D. is an associate professor at the Faculty of Education, University of Malaya. She was previously Head of Department, Language and Literacy Education and a former deputy director at the Centre for Community and Industry Relations at the University of Malaya. She is also a Fulbright scholar (USA, 2006). She has published widely on the topic of second language teaching and learning, second language teacher education and professional development, school-based assessment and content-based instruction.

Fatiha Senom, Ph.D. is a senior lecturer at the Department of Language and Literacy Education, Faculty of Education, University of Malaya. She has published on the issues surrounding the professional development of novice and pre-service ESL teachers. Her research interests include second language teacher education and professional development, teaching English for young learners and qualitative research. She is also an editor for the journal *Issues in Education*.

Routledge Research in Teacher Education

The Routledge Research in Teacher Education series presents the latest research on Teacher Education and also provides a forum to discuss the latest practices and challenges in the field.

For more information about this series, please visit: https://www.routledge.com/Routledge-Research-in-Teacher-Education/book-series/RRTE

Professional Development through Mentoring

Novice ESL Teachers' Identity Formation and Professional Practice

Juliana Othman and Fatiha Senom

Routledge
Taylor & Francis Group

LONDON AND NEW YORK

First published 2020
by Routledge
2 Park Square, Milton Park, Abingdon, Oxon OX14 4RN

and by Routledge
52 Vanderbilt Avenue, New York, NY 10017

Routledge is an imprint of the Taylor & Francis Group, an informa business

First issued in paperback 2021

British Library Cataloguing-in-Publication Data
A catalogue record for this book is available from the British Library

Library of Congress Cataloging-in-Publication Data
A catalog record for this book has been requested

ISBN: 978-1-138-36052-5 (hbk)
ISBN: 978-1-03-209041-2 (pbk)
ISBN: 978-0-429-43309-2 (ebk)

Typeset in Times New Roman
by codeMantra

Contents

Acknowledgements

We are indebted to Katie Peace, the Commissioning Editor, for encouraging us to put in a proposal when we shared our initial thoughts with her and for her positive and prompt responses to it. This book would have never come about without her encouragement to push us through. Finally, we wish to thank the reviewers commissioned by Routledge for their feedback on the book proposal.

1 Introduction

In the past four decades, we have seen the emergence of advances in the field of research in second language teacher education (SLTE) and professional development. The development of SLTE has been impacted by a reconsideration of the knowledge base of the field, a change of perspectives on the nature of teacher learning, a focus on teacher's identity in teacher learning as well as critical perspectives on teacher education.

Research has shown that quality professional development is able to transform teachers' practices and positively influence students' learning (Borko, 2004; Darling-Hammond, 2000; Farrell, 2015; Wright, 2010). This line of research has been closely aligned with work in teacher learning to understand the nature and growth of teachers' professional development. In the context of English as a Second Language (ESL) teacher development, there is a growing need for more effective approaches to enhance the professionalism of ESL teachers. This need emerges as a result of globalization and the spread of English as an international language, which, in turn, led to a growth in demand for English teachers at all levels. In order to be effective teachers, Richards and Farrell (2011) have proposed different dimensions of knowledge and skills that are vital for teacher learners to acquire in SLTE programmes. They argued that teacher learning involves not only acquiring and applying the skills and content knowledge but also developing the identity of a language teacher in a particular context. As such, experts in the field of professional development advocate that teacher professional development (TPD) programme should accommodate to teachers' needs and take into account teacher as learners of their profession in order to provide them opportunities to develop their professional practice.

The understanding of how teachers learn is crucial, as this knowledge is prerequisite for any TPD programme to be effective. Avalos (2011) points out that teachers' professional development is a "complex process which requires cognitive and emotional involvement of teachers individually and collectively" in contexts that are not always conducive for learning (p. 10). Thus, there is a need for more research that explores the complexities of teachers' learning in the professional development contexts (Borko, 2004).

In SLTE, the professional development of English language teachers has progressed from a transmission-oriented approach to a constructivist perspective on how teachers learn how to teach, and what skills and knowledge they need to become effective teachers. The transmission approach assumes that the mere transmission of theoretical knowledge related to content knowledge and language-teaching methodology will lead to teachers' effective classroom practices. On the other hand, the constructivist perspective of teacher and teacher learning sees teachers as active agents of their teaching and learning, and primary sources of knowledge about teaching. The constructivist view also places an importance of teacher inquiry and research throughout teacher education and development programme (Crandall, 2000). This change of perspectives on the nature of teacher learning has been the impetus for a rethinking of the content and delivery of SLTE programmes. Thus, in recent years, teacher education programmes have adopted a 'reflective' and 'inquiry-based' approach to teacher learning.

In more recent years, sociocultural theory has influenced much of the research on teacher education and development (Johnson, 2006, 2009). The sociocultural perspective on teacher learning posits that learning takes place in specific setting and contexts that shape how learning takes place (Richards, 2008). Within this sociocultural perspective, studies have focused on teacher cognition (Woods, 1996) and sociocultural aspects of teacher learning in communities of practice (Lave & Wenger, 1991; Wenger, 1998). In practical terms, this has led to a focus on the process of becoming a member of the teaching community and learning to teach through negotiation and collaborative construction of meanings. This shift in perspective on teacher learning has a major influence in the inquiry into professional learning communities (DuFour, 2004) and teacher collaboration and professional development.

One of the focuses of TPD within the sociocultural perspective is the novice teacher induction programme. Many scholars see it as a vital support system for novice teachers to navigate the early years of their profession, which are characterized by various challenges. Novice teacher induction programme is designed to ease new teachers' transition from their teacher education programme to become professional teachers. Thus, it is imperative for the induction programme to facilitate the novice teachers' process of assimilation into the teaching community and develop positive identities as teachers.

Although literature on novice teachers has been well documented in general education, research in the area of second language teaching is relatively limited (Borg, 2010; Crandall & Christison, 2016; Farrell, 2015; Richards & Pennington, 1998). Research has indicated that a large number of novice teachers leave the profession in the first years (Smith & Ingersoll, 2004) partly due to lack of supportive mentoring in schools. Studies have shown that excellent novice teacher induction programmes facilitate beginning teachers to attain a high standard of professional practice (Hobson, Ashby, Malderez, & Tomlinson, 2009; Wang & Odell, 2002). Britton, Raizen, Paine, and Huntley (2000) assert that induction programme can be viewed as lifeline to encourage "more swimming" and "less sinking" among novice teachers. In the same vein, Ingersoll and Strong (2011) claim that novice teachers who participate in effective induction programme demonstrate successful classroom management and possess better teaching skill. Furthermore, Velez-Rendon (2006) points out the vital role cooperating teachers play in novice teachers' professional development in terms of facilitating their socialization into the profession and providing guidance and serve as a role model to them.

Studies of novice teachers' professional development through mentoring

Mentoring is one of the main components in novice teachers' induction programme. It serves as a bridge between teacher preparation and the in-service teaching, and it assists novice teachers to adjust to the challenges of teaching and to develop into professional practitioners. Second language teacher educators are aware that novice teachers face many issues and challenges in their first years (Faez & Valeo, 2012; Farrell, 2006, 2012; Johnson, 1996). Studies (Brock & Grady, 2007; Smith & Ingersoll, 2004) have shown that mentoring is a significant and effective form of supporting the professional development of novice teachers. There are plenty of research on the values of mentoring especially for the novice teachers.

However, Mann and Tang (2012) argued that most of the studies discuss novice teachers' experience in their first year of teaching 'in one snapshot' (p. 472). Little attention is given to their professional development and transformation during their first year of teaching. In addition, very few studies have focused on close examination of novice teachers' learning experience that takes place during mentoring

(Kardos & Johnson, 2007). Thus, it is valuable to explore the novice ESL teachers' learning experience that takes place while participating in the professional development programme as it would provide a better understanding of what the novice teachers learn from the programme, how this learning is initiated in the induction programme, and also how this learning influences their professional practices.

Research has shown that mentoring enables novice teachers to enhance their content knowledge and pedagogical knowledge by maintaining their role as learners and by gaining benefits from their mentors' competency (e.g. Halai, 2006; Hudson, 2005). Numerous studies (e.g. Halai, 2006; Hobson et. al., 2009; Hudson, 2005; Steers van Hamel, 2004) have addressed the roles of mentoring pertaining to novice teachers' knowledge, practices, and identity formation. However, the examination of teachers' knowledge, practices, and identity formation are conducted separately. Hobson et al. (2009) examined how mentoring supports the capabilities development of novice teachers especially in enhancing their classroom practices. On the other hand, Steers van Hamel (2004) investigates how mentoring strongly influences the formation of novice teachers' identity through the affective relationship formed between the novice teachers and their mentors. Miller (2009) argued that although teachers' thinking, knowing and doing, and identity formation, are enacted in classroom contexts, there is a general paucity of literature that connects all of these dimensions. Therefore, little is known about the relationship between teachers' professional knowledge, teachers' professional practice, and teachers' professional identity.

Furthermore, there has been a great deal of research conducted to explore teacher knowledge in general education and within the TESOL field (e.g. Borg, 2003; Freeman & Johnson, 1998; Golombek, 1998; Meijer, Verloop, & Beijard, 1999; Miller, 2009; Shulman, 1987). Although these studies have been remarkable in extending our understanding of teachers' practical knowledge, there are still very few studies that investigate how teachers' knowledge shapes and is shaped by their identity (Miller, 2009).

According to Kamhi-Stein (2009), most of the research that discuss the identity development of non-native English-speaking teachers during teacher preparation and development programme are conducted in Inner Circle countries such as in the UK, the US, New Zealand, Australia, and Canada, where English is the dominant language. The role of English as a global lingua franca has led to a growing demand of non-native English-speaking teachers in the Outer Circle countries. Hence, there is a need for more research that discuss the identity development of non-native English-speaking teachers during teacher preparation and development programme in an ESL setting in order to inform and enrich the literature corpus on novice non-native teachers' identity from different contexts.

Kiely and Askham (2012) suggest that the understanding of novice teacher learning during a professional development programme can best be understood through the construct of *Furnished Imagination,* which is "an understanding of key elements of the knowledge bases, procedural competence in planning for and managing lessons, a disposition characterised by enthusiasm and readiness, and teacher identity" (p. 509). The fusion of knowledge, procedural awareness and skills, dispositions and identity serves as a way of understanding how teachers construct their professional knowledge, as a way of tracking their professional practice, and as a way of capturing their professional identity formation. Thus, the understanding of novice teachers' learning that takes place during a mentoring programme requires a close examination on the three main elements, namely teacher professional knowledge, teacher professional practice, and teacher professional identity.

Hence, the study discussed in this book aims to address these gaps in the literature by exploring novice ESL teachers' learning during their participation in a mentoring programme in Malaysia named the *Native Speaker Programme.* The study examines how the programme influences novice teachers' professional knowledge, professional practice and professional identity in an English as a Foreign Language (EFL) setting. In this study, we address the following questions:

1 How does the *Native Speaker Programme* contribute to the novice teachers' professional knowledge?
2 How does the *Native Speaker Programme* influence the novice teachers' professional practice as English language teachers at primary schools in Malaysia?
3 In what way does the novice teachers' professional identity formation change after the *Native Speaker Programme*?

The native speaker programme

As an initiative to enhance the professionalism of English language teachers in Malaysia, the Ministry of Education (MOE) introduced and implemented the *Native Speaker Programme* in early 2011. The Ministry of Education aims to improve the proficiency of English language by reforming the existing curriculum and providing sufficient competent teachers as well as quality teaching resources (Ministry of Education, 2012). The MOE has brought in native speakers to help local English teachers in primary schools to enhance their English language mastery level and to improve the teaching and learning strategy based on a belief that the native speaker of English is the best teacher and model of the language use.

The *Native Speaker Programme* is a mentoring programme that aims at enhancing the professionalism of English language teachers in selected primary schools in Malaysia. Under this programme, 376 Native English Speaker (NES) mentors were recruited to train local non-native English teachers at the primary schools. In the mentoring programme at primary school level, the mentors assisted the local ESL teachers to improve their quality of teaching through activities such as TPD courses, observation of teachers' classroom teaching and learning activities, interaction and discussion, collaboration with colleagues as well as co-teaching.

Although the *Native Speaker Programme* aims generally at enhancing the capacity of English language teachers in selected primary schools, it is vital to focus on the influence of this programme on the learning experience of participating ESL primary school teachers, particularly on the novice teachers. Hence, understanding the impact of this mentoring programme must include the voice of those for whom the programme is being implemented. Despite the intricate transition from teacher preparation programme to life in a real classroom experienced by the novice teachers, this concern is not fully addressed in schools in Malaysia as novice teachers are entrusted with similar responsibility as teachers with many years of service.

Therefore, this book aims to address these gaps in the literature by exploring novice ESL teachers' learning during their participation in a *Native Speaker Programme* and by exploring the connection between novice ESL teachers' professional knowledge, practice and identity during their participation in the programme. Furthermore, in the context of SLTE, few studies examined the consequences of pairing native English speaker mentor with non-native English-speaking novice teachers. The study presented in this book examines if the native speaker construct has an impact on the ESL teachers' professional identities development.

Overview of the book

With a reference to case studies in Malaysian context, this book provides an insight into the challenges faced by novice ESL teachers and how mentoring could serve as a strategy to facilitate them transitioning from their teacher education programmes to life in a real classroom.

It also discusses how mentoring can be an effective tool for novice teachers' professional development particularly on their professional knowledge, practice, and identity. It includes a discussion on the theoretical background which views mentoring as a process to novice teachers' development particularly to the teachers' ability to succeed and grow in a specific workplace context. Through its case studies, the book examines both theoretical and practical issues for mentors, teacher educators, policymakers, and administrators in mentoring novice ESL teachers.

In Chapter 1, *Introduction*, we introduce a set of information, which foregrounds this study to enable readers to understand the overall view of the study presented in this book. We outline some of the issues that have emerged in SLTE and professional development in recent years and provide an overview of the research as it relates to these issues. Many of these issues are taken up and elaborated in subsequent chapters in this book. General information on the *Native Speaker Programme*, research questions, and the significance of this study are also articulated.

Chapter 2, *Understanding novice teachers*, gives an account of novice teachers' development. With reference to both current and classic literature on novice teachers, this chapter highlights the challenges in the first years of teaching, Maynard and Furlong's (1995) stages of novice teacher development as well as addressing their need for support. We then provide an overview of studies concerning novice teachers' knowledge, practice, and identity.

In Chapter 3, *The professional development of the ESL teachers*, we present the background knowledge for understanding the discussion of the case studies in Chapters 6–8. In this chapter, we discuss Leung's (2009) concept of *sponsored professionalism* and *independent professionalism* in TPD. Next, we look at teacher professional knowledge, factors influencing teacher's knowledge and teacher learning. A special reference to TPD in Malaysia was made in order to provide the context of this study.

In Chapter 4, *Mentoring*, we present the conceptualization of mentoring as a strategy for supporting novice teachers' transition from their teacher education programme to life as full-fledged teachers. Next, we discuss the conditions of effective mentoring and the impact of mentoring on novice teachers' professional development particularly on their professional knowledge, practice, and identity. This chapter also presents the different mentoring models in teacher education.

In Chapter 5, *The case studies*, we describe the methodological choices that were made for this study. It starts by describing why this research is considered a multiple case study within a qualitative interpretive research design. Next, the contextual background of this study is presented. The chapter further describes the notion of *Furnished Imagination* as the conceptual framework of this study. We also provide background information on the four novice teachers who participated in the case studies. The methods of data collection are then explained, followed by stages and procedures of data analyses.

In Chapter 6, *Enhancing Professional Knowledge through Mentoring*, we discuss four case studies that foreground the research on supporting novice ESL teachers' professional development through mentoring. It presents a comprehensive discussion on four case studies pertaining to the impact of mentoring on novice teachers' professional knowledge. Furthermore, this chapter addresses how mentoring bridges the gap between pre-service training and real classroom, and expands teachers' knowledge base, concerning the four case studies and through the juxtaposition with existing literature.

In Chapter 7, *Professional practice development through mentoring*, a thorough discussion on the impact of mentoring on novice teachers' professional practice is presented with reference to the four case studies. Through the comparison between the four case studies and the existing literature, it addresses how mentoring influences novice teachers' classroom management, ways to motivate students, teaching methodology, selection of teaching materials as well as engagement in reflective practice.

Chapter 8, *Professional Identity Formation through Mentoring*, provides an in-depth discussion on the impact of mentoring on novice ESL teachers' professional identity. Based on the four case studies and with reference to existing research, this chapter examines how mentoring inculcates positive values to novice teachers, empowers their self-confidence, promotes positive perception about teaching profession and enhances teacher retention as well as inspires novice teachers to embrace their identity as non-native English teachers.

Finally, in Chapter 9, *Revisiting the novice ESL teachers' mentoring programme*, we address the criticisms on the mentoring programme in Malaysia, with a specific reference to the *Native Speaker Programme*. We also revisit the notion of mentoring novice teachers and highlight the need to rethink the novice ESL teachers' professional development, especially in the Malaysian context. We proposed several initiatives that can be taken into consideration by the relevant stakeholders. This could be valuable for researchers who are interested to explore this niche as well as for practitioners to improve the current practice in SLTE and development.

2 Understanding novice teachers

The term "novice" has frequently been used in studies on beginning teachers. There is no consensus on the precise definition of a novice teacher, but some researchers described a novice as a teacher with less than five years of teaching experience (Freeman, 2001; Kim & Roth, 2011). Farrell (2012), on the other hand, defined novice teachers as teachers who have just started teaching in an educational institution within three years after completion of their teacher education programme. In their first years of teaching, novice teachers are generally involved in the process of learning how to teach. They need to continue their own learning by improving their pedagogy and content knowledge. Kang and Cheng (2014) point out that the early years of teaching are important for novice teachers to "test their beliefs and ideas, expand their teaching strategies, acquire practical knowledge, and formulate their professional identity" (p. 170). Thus, novice teachers need support and guidance to grow as professionals to enable them to achieve a sense of satisfaction from the work they do.

Novice teachers' challenges

There has been general consensus in research about novice teachers having to deal with various challenges and fight for their survival (Kagan, 1992; Melnick & Meister, 2008; Veenman, 1984). Smith and Ingersoll (2004) point that teaching has been viewed as an "occupation that 'cannibalizes its young' and in which the initiation of new teachers is akin to a sink or swim, trial by fire, or boot camp experience" (p. 28). Ewing and Smith (2003) assert that novice teachers have to adapt to teaching environment in school and navigate the rituals and norms of the staffroom culture. In an earlier study, Gordon and Maxey (2000) reported that among six contextual challenges that novice teachers face include difficult work assignment, unclear goals, inadequate availability of resources, being in isolation, role conflict, and reality shock. In addition, novice teachers are expected to deliver equal amount of work as experienced teachers at the beginning of their career (Weasmer & Woods, 2000).

Studies from the field of mainstream education have identified that novice teachers often find themselves inadequately prepared for the challenges that they need to face during first years in the classroom. Among the serious problems encountered by novice teachers, according to Kagan (1992), are that new teachers do not have the requisite knowledge of classroom procedure to understand the complex interrelationship among management, behaviour, and academic tasks. This lack of knowledge prevents new teachers from focusing on student learning; instead, they are preoccupied with their own behaviour as they try different workable procedures. Walker (1993) reported that novice teachers' greatest concerns include classroom management interactions, effective teaching of language arts, and ability to work with groups of varying sizes. In another study, Britt (1997) found the greatest concern to be these four: time management, discipline, parent involvement, and preparation. Likewise, Melnick and Meister (2008) reported that novice teachers were concerned with their inability to deal with discipline, diverse needs of some students, and being overwhelmed by workload. The teachers talked about time constraints in terms of the amount of time required to plan and implement a lesson, as well as deal with all the paper work.

The challenges of early years of teaching have recently been acknowledged by language education researchers as having a strong influence on the future development of language teachers. Research (Faez & Valeo, 2012; Farrell, 2008; Johnson, 1996; Urmston & Pennington, 2008) has pointed to the gap between the pre-service training of language teachers and the reality of the teaching environment they encounter in their beginning years and the struggle novice teachers face in trying to implement what they have been taught. Richards (1998) posits that novice teachers do not automatically apply the knowledge they received in pre-service training because as teachers they have to construct and reconstruct "new knowledge and theory through participating in specific social contexts and engaging in particular types of activities and processes" (p. 164). Darling-Hammond (2010) also points out that many novice teachers find the transition from teacher education programme to being an in-service teacher overwhelming due to unrealistic demands imposed on them. Novice teachers cannot be considered as finished products because it undermines the process of learning to teach. The process requires sharpening skills and continual learning through inquiry and refinement. Feiman-Nemser (2003) maintains that novice teachers need three to four years to achieve a level of proficiency.

There are few studies that have documented the language teachers' first-year teaching experiences in the TESOL education literature (Farrell, 2006). Richards and Pennington's (1998) study of five novice ESL teachers in Hong Kong secondary schools reported that the teachers abandon the principles of communicative language teaching presented in teacher education programmes and adopt a teacher-centred approach instead. The researcher suggests that heavy workload, large class sizes, and low language proficiency are the factors influencing novice teachers' classroom practices.

Another study that takes into account the TESOL context is Farrell's (2003). This case study examines the challenges experienced by a Singaporean novice teacher during his first year as an English language teacher in his home country. The study also details his experience as he socialized through different phases of Maynard and Furlong's (1995) five stages of novice teacher development. The findings reveal that the participant struggled with "reality shock" as his workload unexpectedly mounted as compared to his practicum experience. He was confronted with two major dilemmas pertaining his context: examination papers grading and his relationship with lower English proficiency students. The novice teacher felt that he received inadequate support as the school in which he taught exhibited the culture of individualism. Consequently, there was a lack of communication with his colleagues and this hindered the opportunity of sharing and cooperating. In terms of Maynard and Furlong's (1995) stages of development, he first entered the school with early idealism, followed by the survival stage where he pursued quick fixes for students' misbehaviours during his lesson. However, he constantly moved back and forth between final three phases: recognizing difficulties, reaching a plateau, and moving on. Then, he started to focus on the quality of his students' learning toward the end of the first year.

In Urmston and Pennington's (2008) study, they found that novice teachers had difficulty in implementing the innovative approaches that they have been exposed to on their teacher education programme due to constraints such as public examinations. Faez and Valeo (2012) reported that novice teachers increased their sense of preparedness as they gained more experience and a sense of efficacy in managing instructional tasks. In a more recent study, Farrell (2016) found that lack of professional support and guidance, feelings of alienation and isolation, and large class sizes are part of challenges that novice teachers faced in their first years of teaching. Jones (2003) suggests that novice teachers need support and guidance in the process of reconciling their personal beliefs and values with realities of teaching as well as developing positive identities as teachers.

Equally challenging is figuring out ways to support and assist novice teachers as they enter the profession. Novice teachers often feel overwhelmed, isolated, and inadequate as teachers (Farrell, 2003, 2006, 2016). Consequently, they develop a survival mentality and learn to cope with their problems. Without support and guidance, novice teachers have been found to adopt "coping survival strategies" which can actually prevent effective instruction from happening and unassisted beginners are also likely to develop negative teaching behaviours.

Need for support

Assisting novice teachers in their professional development towards becoming competent teachers is important in current education system. According to Feiman-Nemser (2001), the first years of teaching influence not only whether novice teachers remain in the profession, but also the kind of teacher they become. Regardless of how effective a teacher education programme has been, novice teachers in their early years would generally face numerous challenges. As mentioned earlier, the challenges come in a variety of forms that include managing challenging student behaviours in the classroom, content knowledge, pedagogy, completing the syllabus, and adapting to the teaching environment.

Smith and Sela (2005) draw attention that teacher education programme does not sufficiently prepare novice teachers for the complex reality they encounter in their early years of teaching. Supporting this view, Lindgren (2005) argues that classroom reality in school can differ greatly from the pre-service training even with effective teacher education programme. Likewise, Murshidi, Konting, Elias, and Fooi (2006) claim that the reality of school-based teaching differs from novice teachers' expectations and this might induce the feeling of shock among them. Novice teachers have to adapt to their teaching environment in school and navigate the rituals and norms of the school culture. They may experience anxiety and emotional distraught and unable to function effectively if they are not provided with support and guidance at the beginning of their career. As Nguyen and Baldauf (2010) argue, "if the realities or problems of beginning teachers are not dealt with constructively and if new teachers are insufficiently supported personally and professionally, it is unlikely that the outcome of their initial professional practice will be predominantly positive" (p. 41).

Hudson and Beutel (2007) reported that well-planned induction programme can assist novice teachers to make successful transition into teaching profession. Numerous professional development initiatives are employed to provide support for novice teachers, one of which is mentoring. Mentoring helps novice teachers to overcome the challenges of teaching and develop into professional educators, and offers a bridge between teacher preparation and the remaining of their career. Wang and Odell (2002) argue that in order to promote effective teacher learning, mentors must provide support to novice teachers in addressing problems relating to their current classroom practice and teaching. Mentors also need to examine novices' prior dispositions about teaching, learning and students, and in helping novices develop alternative good teaching practices through practical experiences in the context of the classroom. According to Brock and Grady (2007), during the first years of teaching, new teachers tend to search for immediate and concrete solutions to the problems they encounter in the classroom. Hence, mentoring programmes play a major role in assisting the novice teachers by providing them authentic learning experiences that are relevant to their personal and professional interest, which they can apply to their immediate work setting.

Studies have indicated that some of the high-priority needs of novice teachers include classroom management, receiving appropriate advice on school culture, using effective instructional strategies or methods, assessing student progress, differentiating student learning, and emotional support (Faez & Valeo, 2012; Farrell, 2006; Veenman, 1984; Richards & Pennington, 1998). Le Maistre and Pare (2010) point out that through quality mentoring, novice teachers can develop a repertoire of strategies for dealing with the practicalities and complexities associated with contextual school and teaching situations.

In a similar vein, Ingersoll and Strong (2011) argue that novice teachers who received some type of induction had higher job satisfaction, increased self-efficacy, enhanced practices, commitment or retention. Thus, it is imperative for schools to provide a good induction programme so as to facilitate the process of assimilation into the new working environment. An effective induction programme could also increase the retention of novice teachers, promote their personal and professional well-being, improve teaching performance, and transmit the school culture and education system to them.

Novice teachers' development

Teaching is one of the few professions in which a novice is expected to assume full responsibility from the first day on the job. The transition from a student teacher to a teacher of students is a challenging and difficult journey. It is widely recognized that novice teachers need support in their first few years of teaching (Darling-Hammond, 2010; Le Maistre & Pare, 2010) as they struggle to survive in their work environment.

Maynard and Furlong (1995, p. 12) posit that novice teachers go through five stages of teacher development of beginning teachers: (1) early idealism, (2) survival, (3) recognizing difficulties, (4) reaching a plateau, and (5) moving on. In the first stage, early idealism, the beginning teachers reject the image of the older cynical teacher and strongly identify with the students. Then, in the survival stage, the beginning teachers feel overwhelmed by the complexity of the classroom as they respond to the reality shock of the classroom. Consequently, they opt for quick fix methods to survive the reality shock. The third stage of development, recognizing difficulties, sees that the beginning teachers begin to realize the difficulties of teaching and recognize that teachers are limited in terms of what they can achieve. They also enter a self-doubt stage and question if they really can be teachers. This is followed by the next stage, reaching a plateau, where beginning teachers begin to cope well with the routines of teaching. In spite of this, resistance to trying new approaches and methods is developed since beginning teachers do not want to disturb the newly developed routines. They also tend to focus more on classroom management than students' learning. However, changes can be seen in the fifth stage, moving on, as the beginning teacher gives more emphasis on the quality of students' learning. Maynard and Furlong (1995) argue that a lot of support is needed by the beginning teacher at this stage to prevent the hindrance of further development due to possible burnout.

In Moir's (1999) study, she examined how novice teachers mentally perceived and responded to the first year of teaching through various stages. Her research denotes that during the first phase, *anticipation phase*, novice teachers have idealistic view of teaching and this phase lasts through the beginning weeks of the first year until they get accustomed to the routine of being a teacher. However, in the second phase, novice teachers become overwhelmed by the challenges that they need to face and experience a *survival phase* where they struggle to cope with the demands of their workload. Moir (1999) maintains that during this phase, new teachers are more likely to concentrate on the routine teaching aspects. During the third phase, *disillusionment*, novice teachers begin to question their dedication and their capability in teaching and the duration and intensity of this phase are different for each novice teacher. Beginning teachers gain confidence and learn to develop new coping strategies during the fourth phase, *rejuvenation*. Moir (1999) asserts that new teachers will finally begin to reflect on the quality of their teaching as they enter the final phase, *reflection*. During this phase, novice teachers start to anticipate in different strategy in the future. Moir (1999) stresses "recognizing the stages that new teachers go through gives us a framework within which we can begin to design support programmes to make the first year of teaching a more productive experience for our new colleagues" (p. 23).

Novice teachers' knowledge, practice and identity

Studies on novice teachers raise a multitude of issues that are mainly focused on learning to teach and classroom knowledge (Gatbonton, 2008; Tsang, 2004). These studies show that the first year of teaching has a significant influence on novice teachers' future careers.

In a Chinese context, Tsang's (2004) case study investigated how the personal practical knowledge of three non-native ESL pre-service teachers had an impact on their interactive decision-making. Results of the study shed light on personal practical knowledge with reference to interactive decisions and teachers' other decision-making processes.

In another study, Gatbonton's (2008) study investigated the influence that teaching experience plays a role in building pedagogical knowledge of novice teachers. The study's focus was to explore what categories of knowledge of pedagogical content the participants internalized after completing a training programme. The pedagogical knowledge of the novice teachers was examined in three dominant categories: language management, i.e. how to handle language input and student output, procedural issues, and student handling. The researcher found that novice teachers seem to be able to acquire the dominant categories of pedagogical knowledge despite a few years of training and little teaching experience.

In a more recent study, Kang and Cheng (2014) investigated the development of cognition by EFL novice teachers during the process of learning to teach in the workplace through an in-depth case study. This study is insightful in that it provided an understanding about novice teacher knowledge in an EFL context.

These studies have provided useful insights into novice teachers' knowledge of teaching in the beginning of their profession. Other research focuses on the impact of the early years of teaching on novice teachers' career and how their teaching experiences shape their professional identity and future practices. Wenger (1998) posits that learning is crucial to identity construction because it "transforms who we are and what we can do" (p. 215). Pitton (2006) points out that "the success of new teachers is critically linked to their first teaching experiences and the opportunities they are given to talk through issues they face in the classroom" (p. 2). Studies generally indicate that novice teachers' identities as English language teaching professionals are shaped by teacher development programmes that they participated. Crandall and Christison (2016) argue that part of "being a second language teacher involves the development of a teacher identity, identifying with language teaching as a profession, and, over time, becoming the type of teacher one desires to be" (p. 12).

Studies (e.g. Kanno & Stuart, 2011; Xu, 2012) have indicated that transition of identities is not quick and smooth; rather, the process is full of disruptions and it is through the sustained teaching experience that they come to develop their identities as language teachers. Similarly, Mann and Tang's (2012) study investigates the influence of mentoring on novice teachers' professional development, support, and socialization. They reported that mentors play an important role in supporting novice teachers and argue that emotional support is given to them as "important survival and identity building mechanism" (p. 487).

In light of the struggle experienced by many novice teachers in forming an identity as legitimate ELT professionals due to their non-native linguistic position, some researchers (Golombek & Jordan, 2005; Zacharias, 2010) have focused on the role of teacher development programmes in establishing and promoting their positive self-identification.

Novice teachers in Malaysia

Although the literature corpus on novice teachers has been documented in Asian countries such as Hong Kong and Singapore, little is known about the struggles faced by novice ESL teachers in the Malaysian context (Ibrahim, Mohamod, & Hj Othman, 2008). A nationwide large-scale study (Ministry of Higher Education & Ministry of Education, 2006) on the readiness of novice teachers' professionalism provides some general ideas on the challenges that novice teachers from various fields faced during their first years. The findings of the study reveal that the 910 respondents report facing a moderate amount of problems pertaining to curriculum specifications, resources, teaching preparation, classroom teaching, classroom management, interpersonal relationship, assessment and evaluation, school, administration and service policies, and co-curriculum. An in-depth examination of this data found that the novice teachers participating in the survey of the study rated students' low English proficiency as the most frequent problem they faced during their first years of teaching.

This nationwide large-scale study (Ministry of Higher Education & Ministry of Education, 2006) also employed structured interviews to explore novice teachers' socialization experience. Qualitative data on the socialization problems faced by the novice teachers were categorized into four groups, namely problems concerning students, school community, teaching profession, and parents. The novice teachers in the study informed that among the problems concerning the students include lack of interest in learning, illiteracy, misbehaviour and lack of discipline, and a negative attitude towards learning English. In terms of problems concerning the school community, the novice teachers in the study reported that they were struggling with the burden of teaching assignments and clerical work, new leadership roles, high expectations, lack of support and guidance, isolation, and school politics. Furthermore, the novice teachers noted that among the problems concerning the teaching profession that they faced include inadequate and irrelevant teaching preparation course, fatigue, time-consuming and tedious teaching preparation and lesson planning as well as difficulty in applying theory to practice. The novice teachers also found that they were struggling with high expectations from the parents. Despite these struggles, the novice teachers in the interview consider the challenges to be valuable experience, which they can learn from. They found that positive and rewarding factors such as genuine interest in becoming a teacher, students' good performance and interest in learning as well as support and guidance from colleagues and school administrators motivated them to remain in the profession and continue learning to be effective teachers.

More recent studies (Goh & Wong, 2014; Kabilan & Veratharaju, 2013; Senom, Zakaria, & Ahmad Shah, 2013) have also examined the struggles faced by novice teachers. Kabilan and Veratheraju's (2013) study reported that ESL novice teachers of secondary school were not provided with professional development courses in their first three years despite their readiness to undergo such training. Likewise, Senom et al. (2013) suggested for a more effective structures of teacher professional development to ensure smooth transition from pre-service training to life in a real classroom.

3 The professional development of ESL teachers

The growing demand of highly qualified and quality English teachers in the world today has turned English as a Second Language (ESL) teaching into a challenging profession. As such, there is an increasing demand for more effective approaches to teachers' preparation and professional development (Burns & Richards, 2009). Richards (2008) rightly points out that English teachers are "part of a worldwide community of professionals with shared goals, values, discourse, and practices but one with a self-critical view of its own practices and a commitment to a transformative approach to its role" (p. 161).

Effort towards enhancing English teacher professionalism in ensuring quality teaching and learning is an important agenda in the field of second language teacher education (SLTE). The term *professionalism* is commonly used to refer to practitioners' knowledge, skills, and conduct. Leung (2009) coins the term *sponsored professionalism* to refer to institutionally endorsed and publicly heralded definition of professionalism whereas *independent professionalism* for more individual-oriented notion of professionalism. He argues that it is important for SLTE to find a balance between these two forms of professionalism. *Sponsored professionalism* refers to a form of professionalism that is arranged and defined by regulatory bodies and professional associations to promote professional action and education improvement. *Sponsored professionalism* is usually acknowledged by those bodies and associations or political authorities to represent teachers collectively; however, it does not automatically speak for an individual's views on professionalism as different teachers may have different views based on their experience and practical knowledge. Different forms of the expression of *sponsored professionalism* can be seen in many examples of professional development practices. The examples listed by Leung (2009, p. 50) include but is not limited to the requirement for student-teachers to enrol in certain subjects, the obligation for teachers to have a certain type and level of disciplinary knowledge and experience as outlined by the regulatory bodies, teaching quality inspection menus, and quasi-judicial decisions related to teacher misconducts,

Obviously, sponsored language teacher professionalism has been interpreted differently at different times, in different places, and by different authorities. Nevertheless, this form of professionalism possesses its own values as public statements on *sponsored professionalism* serve as guidelines for the practitioners as they highlight and define formally, what the teachers have to know and do and simultaneously assist in designing the content of professional education programmes. Leung (2009) asserts that public statements on *sponsored professionalism* are able to publicize the epistemic and value preferences employed by a specific authority and professional body. This is crucial as there has always been a strong policy preference for measurable accountability in public service, and they inform the ways certain education-related matters are perceived and used in the world.

Although *sponsored professionalism* weighs such values and importance, it will not suffice and has to be complemented by *independent professionalism*. Unlike *sponsored professionalism*, *independent professionalism* concerns more than just a particular view by regulatory bodies, professional associations, or political authorities. This is because *independent professionalism* encourages practitioners to make inquisitive and critical analysis on mandated requirements and to consider the emerging developments in the world into their professional practice via engaging in reflexive examination of their own beliefs and action and compare it with the handed-down requirements. Leung (2009) stresses the importance of engaging in reflexive examination, which is to turn our thinking or action on itself hence making it an object available for self-examination, as the core element in *independent professionalism*. It involves a careful and critical examination of the assumptions and practices entrenched in *sponsored professionalism* by juxtaposing it with discipline-based knowledge and wider social values, and to make appropriate change and action for improvement. Apparently, this process will eventually require teachers to make a conscious personal choice that is either to comply with the handed-in requirements or to question their educational, pedagogic, and social validity.

Evidently, as compared to *sponsored professionalism*, *independent professionalism* encourages teachers to engage in more authentic and individual-oriented professional development. Much of the discussion in this book will address this dimension of professionalism.

Teacher professional knowledge

There are many constructions of knowledge in the field of education. In SLTE, constructions of knowledge include practical knowledge (Elbaz, 1983), personal practical knowledge (Clandinin & Connelly, 1987), scripts and schema (Clark & Peterson, 1986), and teachers' talking and walking (Mena Marcos & Tillema, 2006). Richards (2008) posits knowledge base in SLTE in two notions. The first notion is *knowledge about*, which he refers to as *explicit knowledge* that teachers have about language and language teaching principles, which are very similar to Shulman's content knowledge. This type of knowledge consists of academic content and methodology course such as language analysis, discourse analysis, phonology, and curriculum development that guide language teachers to teach. In Wallace's (1991) term, it is known as teachers' *received knowledge* that includes the theoretical subject matter and pedagogy content received during the preparatory teaching training stage. Next, is the notion of *knowledge how*. It denotes the *implicit knowledge* that language teachers acquired from the experience gained in the classroom and what works best for them at the moment (Shulman, 1987; Wallace, 1991). It comprised their beliefs, theories, and knowledge (Richards, 2008). Despite various terminologies, all of the constructions of knowledge highlight and recognize the capability of teachers to construct their own knowledge base for teaching.

In the context of the present study, the term 'teacher professional knowledge' employs the definition of Personal Practical Knowledge which Clandinin and Connelly (1987) have characterized as a "moral, affective, and aesthetic way of knowing life's educational situations" (p. 59). Clandinin (1992) has described personal practical knowledge (PPK) as follows:

> It is knowledge that reflects the individual's prior knowledge and acknowledges the contextual nature of that teacher's knowledge. It is a kind of knowledge carved out of, and shaped by, situations; knowledge that is constructed and reconstructed as we live out our stories and retell and relive them through processes of reflection. (p. 125)

Different studies define PPK differently, although they share some likeness. For example, teachers' PPK in Borg's (2003, p. 81) study is incorporated in a general framework of teacher cognition and described as "what teachers know, believe and think". Elbaz (1983, p. 5) suggests that teachers' PPK "encompasses first-hand experience of students' learning styles, interests, needs, strengths and difficulties, and a repertoire of instructional techniques and classroom management skills". On the other hand, Connelly and Clandinin (1988, p 25) explain that teachers' PPK is "found in the teacher's practice. It is, for any teacher, a particular way of reconstructing the past and the intentions of the future to deal with the exigencies of a present situation". In contrast, according to Feiman-Nemser and Floden (1986), teachers' PPK is the practitioner's personal understanding of the practical circumstances of their work environments.

Factors influencing teachers' knowledge

Borg (2003) suggests that numerous contextual sources contribute to the formation of teachers' practical knowledge. These include professional development programme coursework, teaching experience, knowledge about subject matter, apprenticeship of observation as a learner, personalities, engagement in reflective practice, and the school setting (Borg, 2003). Grossman's (1990) study on English teachers' pedagogical content knowledge proposes a conceptual framework that considers the factors influencing the development of teachers' pedagogical content knowledge. Among the factors that influence teachers' pedagogical content knowledge development as proposed by Grossman (1990) include apprenticeship of observation as learners in secondary, high school, and undergraduate classes, competency in subject matter knowledge, teacher education, and classroom experience.

Meijer, Verloop, and Beijard (1999), in their study to recognize the patterns found in 13 experienced language teachers' practical knowledge underscoring the teaching of reading comprehension, defined six background sources that were expected to shape the content of language teachers' practical knowledge: "a) personal characteristics, b) frequency and nature of reflection, c) prior education, d) years of experience (in teaching), e) the language taught, and f) the school context" (p. 61).

Research in second language education and applied linguistics has recognized the potential of prior experiences of language teachers to influence their knowledge of teaching and practice by scrutinizing the relation between teacher knowledge and prior language learning experiences. Borg (2003) asserts that there is sufficient indication that teachers' experiences as learners can shape teachers' cognition about teaching and learning. The establishment of the cognitions through language learning experience also forms the base of early conceptualizations of L2 teaching during teacher education. In addition, according to the study, the language learning experiences continue to influence teachers in many ways throughout their careers.

Another source that contributes to the formation of language teachers' knowledge is their teaching experience as professionals. Nespor's (1987) study on the role of teachers' beliefs in shaping their professional practice provided a categorized framework on teachers' beliefs that include a category, which is related to teachers' prior experiences – episodic structure. Nespor (1987, p. 320) discovered that "A number of teachers suggested that critical episodes or experiences gained earlier in their teaching careers were important to their present practices". Likewise, Moran's (1996) study documented how a participant who is a Spanish teacher related her experience as a Spanish language learner with her professional practice and how she was influenced by her teaching experience which was facilitated by her students' reactions. All of these experiences transformed her classroom instruction. Similarly, Ulichny's (1996) study documented how her participant's prior experience as an ESL teacher shaped her educational beliefs in her classroom practices. The findings suggested by the cited studies indicate that the teachers' experiences both as second language learners and as teachers are potentially powerful in shaping their professional practice as teachers. Whether they are constructive or destructive, these accumulated experiences play a central role in shaping teachers' classroom instruction.

Teacher learning

Research shows that different contexts, educational discourse, and epistemologies lead to diversity of approaches in teacher learning. In 1970s and earlier, English language teacher learning took place in various teacher-training forms such as short courses like Royal Society of the Arts Certification of Teaching English as a Foreign Language to Adults (RSA-CTEFLA), and higher education like certification and degrees which involved teachers learning merely about language, literature, culture studies, and classroom teaching. Then, the field of Teaching English to Speakers of Other Language (TESOL) was introduced, and the scope of teacher preparation of this field involves teacher learning about grammar and applied linguistics, learners, second language acquisition, and teaching methodologies. With the introduction of TESOL and series of publication by Richard and Nunan on SLTE in the 1990s, there was also a shift in teacher learning. SLTE is not only about what teachers 'know' in ensuring effective second language learning, but also about what they 'do'. Hence, the SLTE field begins to focus on teachers' practice. Since individuals define themselves by their practice in accordance with Lave and Wenger (1998), recent SLTE programmes begin to focus on the concept of identity as an integral part of teacher learning. Additionally, as SLTE begins to address the contexts in which the language learning takes place, teacher learning is arranged in the forms of short courses and in situ professional development programme organized by their workplaces (Freeman, 2009).

Avalos (2011) in her review of teacher professional development over ten years (2000–2010) notes that the core of the studies in this area is the "understanding that professional development is about teachers' learning, learning how to learn, and transforming their knowledge into practice for the benefit of their students' growth" (p. 10). As Johnson (2009) argues, language teacher education can no longer "view L2 teaching as a matter of simply translating theories of second language acquisition into effective instructional practices, but as a dialogic process of co-constructing knowledge that is situated in and emerges out of participation in particular contexts" (p. 21).

Teacher learning is an important aspect of professional development. The understanding of how teachers learn is essential (Johnson, 2009), and this knowledge is prerequisite for any teacher professional development programmes to be effective. However, teacher learning has been defined as an "unstudied problem" since the 1980s in general education (Clark & Peterson, 1986) as well as in language education (Freeman, 1996). Teacher education and professional development has long been characterized by "training" or "teaching" people how to do the work of teaching. The professional literature of language teaching is stocked with stories of the best methods and classroom practice, leaving the rich and complex teacher learning process unquestioned (Freeman, 1996). Professional development is expected to influence teacher practice in a way that enhances student learning and increases student achievement. However, there is not much research deeply validating what type of professional development experiences teachers need to produce a positive impact on student achievement, or how much of this impact is a result of effective professional development (Knapp, 2003).

In examining the impact of a short teacher training course in TESOL on teacher learning, Kiely and Askham (2012) propose *Furnished Imagination* as the key construct that provides theoretical framework for the study. Using telephone or Skype interviews, the study looked at the impact of a short teacher training course in TESOL on 27 novice teachers teaching in different countries in Europe, North America, and Asia. The study examined the impact of the course on an aspect of teacher learning, which is the extent to which novices are ready for work. Novice teachers' readiness for work is constructed as *Furnished Imagination*, which refers to the novice teachers' sense of belonging in the world of TESOL. The study found that the *Furnished Imagination* of novice teachers consists of knowledge, procedural awareness, skills, dispositions, and a TESOL identity. Kiely and Askham (2012) assert that through the combination of knowledge, procedural awareness, skills, dispositions and identity, *Furnished Imagination* operates as a way of understanding teacher learning, as a way of tracking professional learning, as a way of capturing teacher learning as professional identity formation in sociocultural terms, and as a way of validating learning within TESOL courses.

Teacher professional development in Malaysia

In an effort to raise the standards and quality of Malaysian education system, the Ministry of Education (MOE) launched the National Education Blueprint (2013–2025). Central to this blueprint is the strategy to enhance teachers' professionalism. This includes not only teachers' knowledge, skills and experience, but also their spiritual, social, and financial capitals. In addition, the Ministry also introduced the Malaysia Teacher Standard (MTS) in 2009 to further enhance the ongoing effort to improve teacher professionalism. The MTS serves as a guideline for teachers to develop professional values, knowledge and understanding while acquiring the relevant skills in teaching (Chapman, 2009). In addition to this general guideline, which apply to all teachers, a specific standard for English language teaching was introduced in 2012. The Pedagogy Standards for English Language Teachers (PSELT) serve as a tool to measure the quality of English language teaching among teachers at different stages of their career and to guide the training and professional development of those teachers.

In 2010, the Malaysian Ministry of Education implemented a comprehensive novice teacher induction programme as part of an effort to increase the quality of its teachers. The New Teacher Development Program was designed to provide support to novice teachers throughout their first year. Novice teachers will undergo the programme, which aims to induce them with excellent work culture and guide them towards performing tasks and responsibilities more systematically. This programme is mandated for all novice teachers and focuses on Continuous Professional Development (CPD). Novice teachers must serve between one and three years as interim teachers before their formal confirmation into the teaching profession. During these early years, novice teachers are evaluated through a variety of assessments, including in-service training courses organized by the MOE.

Novice teacher induction in Malaysia is school-based where schools need to organize the programme in line with a Novice Teacher Induction module prepared by the MOE. The induction programme comprises four key components, namely orientation, mentoring, professional development, and evaluation and assessment. The programme runs for a year and starts when the novice teacher joins the school. Novice teachers will be mentored by experienced teachers, who would provide guidance on good teaching practices and work culture. This programme involves mentoring as a form of job-embedded professional development component for guiding and supporting novice teachers.

In Malaysia, teacher professional development programmes centred on *sponsored professionalism* through centralized professional programmes such as seminars, courses, and workshops conducted by the MOE. For instance, as an effort to increase the quality of teachers in Malaysia, the MOE implemented New Teacher Development Programme to support novice teachers in Malaysia. Novice teachers will undergo the programme with the objective of inducing novice teachers with "excellent work culture and gearing them towards performing tasks and responsibilities more systematically" (MOE, 2010). There is little evidence on the existence of *independent professionalism*, which is developed through socially and politically sensitive awareness of professionalism on the part of teachers themselves.

In a case study on ESL teachers' professional development in three primary schools in Malaysia, Mohd Sofi Ali (2008) reported that the prevalent form of professional development in the schools was unstructured and restricted in scope, and thus failed to some extent to provide teachers with the relevant required professional skills and practice. This is because ESL teachers developed their teaching skills and competence merely through their initial education at teacher training colleges, an informal apprenticeship, and years of teaching experience in the school besides relying on their experience as students and by emulating their former teachers as role models. In addition, they learned about their professional roles and related skills intuitively by talking to colleagues and working with other teachers.

In addition, Mohd Sofi Ali (2008) in his case study asserts that the only 'planned' approach to ESL teacher professional development was through in-service courses initiated by the MOE and its professional divisions. In-service courses required ESL teachers to leave schools for a certain period to attend courses, which were believed to enhance teachers' existing qualifications, to assist teachers in areas that they perceived to be challenging, and to further enhance teachers' existing skills. Then, the ESL teachers were expected to share the information with their colleagues in the schools by conducting in-house training sessions upon returning to their respective schools. However, Mohd Sofi Ali (2008) argues that the in-house training sessions rarely occurred in the primary schools. He states that the in-service courses have several limitations because some courses in his case study were considered irrelevant, impractical, and redundant. Thus, there was a mismatch between the needs of teachers and the content of the courses. Moreover, those courses were too theoretical and not applicable especially in the context of English as a foreign language. In addition, the role played by experts outside the school was emphasized; thus, teachers did not consider themselves or their colleagues as experts in their own school and consequently, mistrust among the teachers for internal teacher experts occurred. Furthermore, only a limited number of teachers were given the opportunity to attend those courses since the number of places available depended on the allocation of funds. He also argues that the provision of the course was unsystematic and unplanned with providers determined choices; thus, the locus control of teachers' professional development remained with the Ministry. He added that the cascading model of in-service activities that encourages teachers to disseminate information received to colleagues through in-house training was not implemented effectively due to time constraints, work constraints, and other priorities.

In a more recent study, Kabilan and Veratharaju (2013) reported that Malaysian teachers prefer professional development programme that emphasizes their pupils' needs as well as their own professional needs and interests. The researchers suggested that the Ministry should assist the schools and teachers to take more responsibility to plan, develop, implement, and assess their own professional development programme. They argued that professional development is not only an ongoing process that contributes towards personal growth of teachers, but also an integral element in improving the quality of schools.

Jamil's (2014) study on professional development highlighted the need for an ongoing effort that contributes towards teachers' personal growth and integral element in improving the quality of schools. The researchers also argue for suitable programmes that cater to the teachers' needs. Likewise, Vikaraman, Mansor, and Hamzah (2017) point out that the existing professional development programmes in Malaysia to be "lacking in follow-up support programs, not continuous, one-shot programmes and does not promote collaboration" (p. 161). Furthermore, the programmes are reported to be inflexible, time-consuming, and do not promote collaborative activities or supplementary support after the programmes.

All these are perhaps due to the implementation of the traditional approach of teachers' professional development. Consequently, workshops, seminars, courses, and conferences become predominant forms of professional development practices available in Malaysia. In contrast, recent trends of teacher professional development in other countries such as the United Kingdom, the United States, Australia, and Japan highlight on alternative professional development structures that provide teachers with the platform for self-directed, collaborative, inquiry-based learning, which is directly relevant to teachers' classrooms that recognize teachers' informal social and professional networks as powerful sites for professional learning (Johnson, 2009, p. 25). These alternative structures include teacher inquiry seminars, peer coaching, cooperative development, teacher study groups, narrative inquiry, lesson study groups, and critical friends groups. Such alternative structures encourage teachers to engage in ongoing, in-depth, and reflective examinations of their teaching practices and their students' learning by recognizing the critical role that context plays in teacher learning and L2 teaching (Rogers, 2002) while embracing the processes of teacher socialization that occurs in classrooms, schools, and the wider professional communities where teachers work.

Therefore, in order to ensure ESL teaching in Malaysia benefits from the alternative structures of teacher professional development, there is a need for the educational environment in Malaysia to pursue this current trend as well. Besides, the adoption of these alternative structures will address the importance of *independent professionalism* as a crucial part to the prevailing forms of teacher professional development programmes in Malaysia, which generally pivot around *sponsored professionalism*.

4 Mentoring

Mentoring programmes have now become a dominant part of teacher induction that both terms are being used interchangeably. Mentoring has been widely employed as part of an induction process for helping novice teachers adjust to the challenges of teaching and develop them into quality educators. It offers a bridge between teacher preparation and the remainder of an educator's career. Hobson, Ashby, Malderez, and Tomlinson (2009) define mentoring as

> the one-to-one support of a novice or less experienced practitioner by a more experienced practitioner, designed primarily to assist the development of the mentee's expertise and to facilitate their introduction into the culture of the profession and into the specific local context.
>
> (p. 207)

In the context of mentoring novice teachers in the field of second language teacher education, Malderez (2009, p. 260) refers to mentoring as a "process of one-to-one, workplace-based, contingent and personally appropriate support for the person during their professionalization acclimatization (or integration), learning, growth, and development". In addition, mentoring of novice language teachers needs to occur in the workplace and deals with the authenticities of the particular context that include the particular school, child, and teacher, as well as within particular settings.

Studies have shown that mentoring is an effective solution for teacher retention problems and helping novice teachers increases their confidence, ability, and development as educators (Feiman-Nemser, 2001; Smith & Ingersoll, 2004). Through mentoring process, novice teachers gain confidence through supportive feedback given by their respective mentors. Malderez (2009, p. 260) views mentoring process as "being supportive of the transformation or development of the mentee and of their acceptance into a professional community".

Phillips-Jones (2001) characterized mentors as "experienced people who go out of their way to help a mentee clarify her vision and then help her build the skills to reach them" (p. 21), who take on the roles of coach, learning broker, accountability partner, cheerleader, and sounding board. Additionally, mentors have been described as guides, facilitators, gurus, friends, and mothers who provide support and challenge, explain, and protect (Daloz, 1986). Thus, mentors are often expected, indeed, required to assume multiple roles that include coaching, exposure, challenging work, role modelling, and the encouragement of reflection. Mentors are also individuals who provided mentees with knowledge, advice, challenge, and support (Johnson & Huwe, 2003).

Mentoring models in teacher education

Mentoring practices can be understood in relation to various models of mentoring. Among the different models of mentoring developed in teacher education, we focus on a model proposed by Cochran-Smith and Paris (1995) which characterizes mentoring as either knowledge transmission or knowledge transformation that relates to the discussion of our study. These models will be discussed in this section.

Knowledge transmission model

The knowledge transmission model proposed that mentors perceive their role as expert teachers and transmit their knowledge to teachers in the form of lectures. This knowledge transmission model is based on behaviourism theories of learning which conceptualize learning as the acquisition of knowledge provided by experts. Mentors from this perspective provide novice teachers with instructional techniques and skills, and familiarize them with the contexts and cultures of their work, in particular, teaching situations. This model depends on a mentor's level of skill and knowledge because a novice teacher is expected to be passive recipients of information.

Knowledge transformation model

The knowledge transformation model is based on the premise that teacher mentoring is a continuing process of collaborative inquiry into teaching practice. Learning is viewed as an active process that takes place in a community of practice (Lave & Wenger, 1991). Both mentors and novice teachers share and generate new knowledge from their work through active interaction with the people and resources with which they worked. Novice teachers' professional interaction enables them to expand their teaching repertoires and improves their understandings of their teaching practices. Instead of being passive recipients of knowledge (Richards & Farrell, 2005), novice teachers actively make their own sense of ideas and theories with which they are presented in ways that are personal to them. Development is expected to occur when new information is related to prior practices and beliefs to be either confirmed or challenged depending on individual perceptions and behaviours. The knowledge of teaching developed in this mentoring model is expected to transform the novice teachers' existing practice of teaching and adapt to different teaching contexts.

In this model, the mentor is viewed as an expert and the novice teachers as apprentices whose involvement in the community of practice enables them to acquire certain beliefs and behaviours associated with that particular community. During this process, the novice teacher becomes more active, engaged within the culture, and ultimately embraces the role of an expert. Social interaction and collaboration are regarded as the most important elements of this model and are seen as the medium that allows novice teachers to be involved in a "community of practice" (Lave & Wenger, 1991). Within this framework, mentors are not viewed as transmitters of new knowledge but as facilitators of new knowledge and as facilitators of learning by encouraging reflection, providing feedback on teaching practices, and collaborating on ways to improve.

Conditions for effective mentoring

In her overview of related scholarships on mentoring over the past decade, Delaney (2012, p. 187) argued that "a clear understanding of mentors' roles in this new language teacher education paradigm is key to successful mentoring". Additionally, there is a need for research on ESL mentoring to provide a better understanding on the effective roles of ESL mentor (Brown, 2001; Kissau & King, 2014). Hudson, Skamp, and Brooks (2005) advocate five factors in ensuring effective mentoring: personal attributes, system requirements, pedagogical knowledge, modelling, and feedback.

Personal attributes

Mentors' personal attributes such as personal and interpersonal skills are crucial in engaging with their mentees. These attributes could help mentors to maintain a strong and trusting relationship with their mentees (Moir, 2009; Udelhofen & Larson, 2003). In many studies (Delaney, 2012; Malderez & Bodoczky, 1999), personal qualities that describe effective mentor include responsible, supportive, and having non-confrontational style. In addition, the establishment of academic and emotional support has been regarded as the fundamental elements of mentoring in numerous studies (Ferrier-Kerr, 2009; Jacobi, 1991; Rajuan, Beijaard, & Verloop, 2007). In addition, studies (Feiman-Nemser, 2001; Maynard, 2000; Rippon & Martin, 2006) show that the establishments of emotional and psychological support are essential in ensuring effective mentoring so that the mentees feel accepted and included.

Pitton (2006) asserted that novice teachers feel tremendously stressed just because they are encountering new experience. Hence, it is important for mentors to address novices' reaction to the new experience and provide them with adequate emotional support. Moreover, a number of studies (Harrison, Dymoke, & Pell, 2006; Johnson, Berg, & Donaldson, 2005) define effective mentor for their willingness to make time for their mentees: by having frequent meetings and being available for the mentees even for informal discussion after the school hours.

Additionally, strong emotional connection between mentors and mentees is essential as a condition for effective mentoring since it promotes scholastic competence and boosts self-esteem among the mentees (Deutsch & Spencer, 2009). On the other hand, distant relationships between mentor and mentees hinder such positive outcomes (Izadinia, 2015).

However, the effectiveness of mentoring does not rely solely on the responsibility of the mentor; indeed, the mentee has equally important roles to play. Johnson and Huwe (2003) suggested that mentees should be emotionally stable, coachable, committed, and similar to their mentor concerning interests and philosophy. Additionally, Portner (2003) described mentees as those who were willing and able to participate, take responsibility, observe, ask, take informed risks, reflect, and give back. More specifically, mentors of student teachers expected their mentees to be willing to listen and learn as a means of extending their professional development, to accept advice and act upon it, and to develop positive relationships with their students (Hayes, 2008).

System requirements

Research has shown that supportive systems are the conditions required for effective mentoring. As novice teachers begin their careers with little knowledge of the school organization and cultural norms, mentors could provide guidance to mentees in navigating the new context in terms of school routines and culture (Achinstein, 2006; Bartell, 2005). In addition, novice teachers may need assistance concerning curriculum, school policies, and student assessment (Hudson, 2007).

As identified by Malderez and Bodoczky (1999), mentors play important roles as 'acculturators' who assist mentees to embrace their profession in their particularized context and as 'supporters' who facilitate mentees in undergoing an emotional change from their pre-service training to real classroom, by imparting necessary knowledge to them.

Pedagogical knowledge

According to Wang and Odell (2002), an effective mentoring practice requires mentors to support novice teachers in addressing problems about their current classroom practice and teaching. In addition, mentors must assist novice teachers in examining novices' prior dispositions about teaching, learning, and students. In order to promote effective teacher learning, mentors should also help novices to develop alternative good teaching practices through practical experiences in the context of the classroom.

These findings were in line with arguments from several researchers (Hobson, 2009; Foster, 1999; Roehrig, Bohn, Turner, & Pressley, 2008) who emphasize the role of mentors as the experts who are able to model excellent professional practice. Moreover, the findings of the study support Abell, Dillon, Hopkins, McInerney, and O'Brien (1995) who asserted that effective mentoring demands mentors to have adequate subject matter knowledge to allow mentees to have 'professional respect' for their mentors.

In terms of motivation, studies (Foster, 1999; Lindgren, 2005; Valenčič, Zuljan, & Vogrinc, 2007) have shown that for mentoring programme to be effective, it needs to cater to the need of the mentees. Hence, mentoring strategies should acknowledge mentees' learning style by providing suitable activities that cater to their needs and preferences.

In addition, research (Jonson, 2002; Martin & Rippon, 2003; Schmidt, 2008) shows that valuable mentoring activities include the collaboration of both mentor and mentee in the process of teaching. This requires them to work together to reach a consensus when planning a lesson as well as to reflect on the conducted activities in positive and constructive ways in order to identify the strengths and weaknesses of the teaching and learning activities and ways to improve the lessons.

Generally, mentoring assists novice teachers in improving their practice classroom (Hobson et al , 2009; Malderez, 2009; Strong, 2009; Orland-Barak, 2014). The findings of Evertson and Smithey's (2000) study on mentor-protégé relationships indicated that mentoring assisted protégés to develop more efficient classroom routine, deliver clearer classroom instruction, enhance students' participation in teaching and learning activities, and reduce students' misbehaviour. In a recent study specifically in the field of second language teacher education, Kissau and King (2014) discovered that beginning teachers without mentors faced difficulty in planning their lesson as compared to teacher with mentor.

Modelling

Darling-Hammond, Holtzman, Gatlin, and Heilig (2005) argue that mentors' modelling of instructional practices is important for novice teachers' development. Moir (2009) who points out that effective mentors are often seen as instructional coaches and models of the best instructional practices themselves further supports this view. The quality of modelling in which mentees have the opportunity to observe and practice could facilitate their pedagogical development (Darling-Hammond, 2006).

Richter et al.'s (2013) study has found that the effectiveness of mentoring programme in creating successful beginning for novice teachers lies on the quality of mentoring strategies rather than its frequency. In addition, mentoring strategies that employ constructivist approach are superior in producing novice teachers who are effective, enthusiastic, satisfied, and contented, as compared to mentoring strategies that employed transmissive approach.

Feedback

The provision of constructive feedback by mentors plays an important role in building mentees' confidence, positive attitudes, and pedagogical skills (Hudson, 2007). Mentors could provide feedback in relation to pedagogical issues such as classroom management, lesson planning, and assessment. Feedback could facilitate novice teachers to reflect on strategies for improving their instructional practices so as to improve their students' learning.

According to Kissau and King (2014), recent literature on mentoring considered the encouragement of communication, teamwork, and reflection between mentees as an important trait of effective mentoring. Likewise, researchers (Hobson et al., 2009; Lee & Feng, 2007; Whisnant, Elliott, & Pynchon, 2005) argued that novice teachers' mentoring would be more effective if it promotes collegial learning culture where the teachers in similar or different schools are given the opportunity to interact with each other.

According to Burton (2009), reflective practice serves as a powerful tool that promotes teachers' lifelong professional development as it allows them to evaluate their teaching in order for them to improve their professional practice. Mentoring has a noteworthy role in the establishment of reflective practice among the teachers (Bates, Drits, & Ramirez, 2011; Feiman-Nemser, 2001; Franke & Dahlgren, 1996; Hobson et al., 2009). Moran and Dallat (1995) argued that mentors assisted mentees in developing their reflective skills in two ways: through demonstrating reflection on their own practice and through promoting the critical thinking skills among the mentees by continually questioning the effectiveness of mentees' practice.

Benefits of mentoring

There has been a consensus in research that effective mentoring practices could facilitate the novice teachers' professional development (Carter & Francis, 2001; Gu & Benson, 2015; Mann & Tang, 2012; Menard-Warwick, 2008). The benefits of mentoring include boosting the confidence and self-esteem, reduced feelings of isolation, improved self-reflection, and professional growth of novice teachers. Smith and Ingersoll's (2004) study points out that mentoring reduces the risk of a novice teacher leaving at the end of her first school year by 30 per cent. Novice teachers report that effective mentoring reduces feelings of segregation, improves self-reliance and self-image, and increases professional development, self-reflection, and critical thinking ability (Hudson et al., 2010).

Other studies have also pointed out the influences of mentoring on novice teachers' improvement in terms of their classroom management skills and capability in managing their time and workloads (Malderez, Hobson, Tracey, & Kerr, 2007; Moor et al., 2005). Furthermore, mentors have been reported to facilitate the socialization of novice teachers, assisting them to cope with norms, standards, and expectations related to teaching (Hobson et al., 2009; Moussu & Llurda, 2008; Wang & Odell, 2002).

Brock and Grady (2007) posit that mentoring programmes are able to provide novice teachers with an authentic learning environment that is based on individual classroom experiences. An authentic learning environment is important for novice teachers as they are searching for immediate, concrete solutions to the problems they encounter within their first years in the classroom. In considering what beginning teachers need from a mentoring programme in learning to teach, Brock and Grady (2007) argue that

> Adults commit to learning when they view something as important and relevant to their personal and professional needs. Beginning teachers want information that they can apply to their immediate work setting. The best chances for professional growth occur when participants perceive a need and the information provided is relevant to their personal and professional interests.
>
> (p. 67)

Evertson and Smithey (2000), in their study of mentor-protégé relationships observed that protégés whose mentors received training sustained "more workable classroom routines, managed instruction more smoothly, and gained student cooperation in academic tasks more effectively" (p. 302). Additionally, the novice teachers who participated in mentoring programme were observed to have fewer student disruptions in their classrooms. Thus, their study suggests that mentoring can assist novice teachers in improving teaching skills in various ways.

Impact of mentoring in relation to novice teachers' knowledge and practice

Several studies (Hobson et al., 2009; Rajuan, Beijaard, & Verloop, 2007) have suggested that mentoring provides support for novice teachers to increase their content knowledge. Halai's (2006) study on novice teachers in Pakistan discovered that despite the incapability of the local teacher preparation programmes to train quality teachers, mentoring was able to enhance the novice teachers' teaching competency. It was found that the novice teachers were able to enhance their content knowledge through mentoring, as they view themselves as learners and through the guidance given by their mentors. In the same way, Hudson (2005) found that novice science teachers who received guidance from their mentors particularly on the enhancement of pedagogical knowledge were more successful as compared to novice science teachers who did not have mentors.

A review article by Hobson et al. (2009) reported that mentoring could have a positive impact on teachers' early teaching experiences. They found that mentoring facilitated the improvement of novice teachers' self-reflection and problem-solving skills. Mentoring programme could also lead to an increased collaboration and collegiality among teachers through the culture of professional support.

In Hong Kong, Mann and Tang (2012) examined four novice English teachers' mentoring process throughout their first year of teaching. The findings showed that mentors made positive impact on the novice teachers' experience when they were given opportunities to collaborate and work on teaching activities together. This is consistent with Smith and Ingersoll's (2004) findings. The influence of mentoring programme on novice teachers' knowledge and practice is also discussed in Reid's (2010) study where the knowledge and meanings constructed by novice teachers within a multi-year, standards-based mentoring programme were examined. The findings of the study suggest that the mentoring programme reinforced the knowledge about various teaching skills such as classroom management, catering to students' needs, and teaching approach. The novice teachers also feel more ready to focus on adjusting their practice to support student learning, but often continue to focus on classroom management, student behaviour, and the problems that arise weekly in their mentoring. These teachers also recognize the importance of the knowledge gained during the mentoring programme, but find it difficult to apply that learning at the level they feel they should.

However, some teachers in Reid's (2010) study did show changes in their practice with a central focus on student learning. The data of the study indicated that the beginning teachers were more likely to examine and adjust their instruction with a focus on student learning and student needs when the mentor scaffolded, or specifically supported, the teachers' learning. The study suggests that mentoring moved beyond merely reflecting the current situation by focusing on prominent future practice and planning specifically how to apply teacher learning to classroom practice. Such scaffolding included helping the beginning teacher identify what changes were needed, working together to plan for implementing those changes, and examining data to determine evidence of the impact of the teachers' choices on students.

Impact of mentoring in relation to novice teachers' identity

Research also points to the impact of mentoring on novice teachers' identity formation (Kanno & Stuart, 2011; Menard-Warwick, 2008;

Trent, 2012; Xu, 2013). Novice teachers experience shifts in identities from students to professional as they go through training programmes and starting teaching positions. Beijaard, Meijer, and Verloop (2004) maintain that teachers' identity is constantly developing and the interaction between teachers' own beliefs and experience is imposed upon the teacher by contextual factors.

The roles of mentoring in novice teachers' identity formation are discussed in Steers van Hamel's (2004) study. Through the exploration of two novice teachers and the influences of formal and informal mentoring relationships on their first year of teaching, her study found beginning teachers were strongly influenced by significant individuals and experiences from their life histories. In addition, the findings of her study suggest that the novice teachers' identity was constructed through their relationships with *informal* mentors to whom they formed an affective relationship due to shared primary discourses. In contrast, formal mentors did not shape the beginning teacher's emerging identity. The findings also suggest that in both case studies, negotiating the relationship with formal mentors actually contributed to the beginning teachers' stress and anxiety. One teacher in her study, Ms Miner, states that her formal mentorship was disastrous. This is because she did not get the help she initially needed at the beginning of the year, and this contributed to her stress. In her study, Steers van Hamel (2004) also highlights the fact that novice teachers were constrained by their individual life histories and institutional biographies. In addition, relationships with veteran colleagues who serve as informal mentors can undermine potentially emancipatory teaching practices learned during teacher education coursework.

Another study that examined the influence of mentoring on novice teachers' identity was conducted by Hayes (2008). In this study, Hayes investigates the ways mentors and novice teachers utilized discourse in negotiating their relationship, the role mentoring relationship played in their co-construction of knowledge about teaching, as well as the ways the knowledge of practice transformed both mentors and novice teachers' individual identities. This research provided evidence of the complexity of mentoring and the ways in which discourses are constructed and changed as they are employed to engage in the activities of mentoring and to transform the identities of the relational partners. The findings of the study imply that although the mentors and novice teachers engaged in many of the same mentoring activities, their identities as mentors, as novice teachers, and as teachers were influenced by the ways in which they negotiated power, as well as the ways in which they positioned each other. In addition, it is also found that mentors and novice teachers who shared power and positioned each other as collaborative partners developed relationships that shaped and transformed their practices and identities. Moreover, the nature of each mentoring relationship was influenced by the discourses that constructed the socio-political context in which the mentors and novice teachers were situated, and the interdependence between the identities of mentor and novice teachers shaped not only the nature of their situated mentoring discourse, but also the ways in which the activities of mentoring were enacted.

Chen, Tigelaar, and Verloop's (2016) review article on the intercultural identities of non-native English teachers reported that numerous contextual factors influence the formation of their identities. These include their previous learning or training experiences, their cross-cultural experience, relationships with students and colleagues, job demands, and socialization. For instance, Menard-Warwick (2008) explores the link between the development of two female teachers' intercultural competence and their transnational life experience. The author found that the teachers developed their bicultural identity through their previous experiences in two cultures. Transnational experiences could be beneficial in developing teachers' intercultural identities.

In Trent's (2012) study, he examined the continuing professional development of English language teachers who participated in a school-university partnership in Hong Kong. The study explores the teachers' negotiation of membership within and across multiple communities. Findings showed that the school-university partnership had an impact on the development of teachers' identity in relation to their engagement with the university consultant and other communities of English language teachers. The identity was negotiated in the joint production of instructional tasks and activities between the teachers and their consultant.

In summary, as research continues to confirm the impact of mentoring programme on novice teachers' knowledge, practices and identity formation, the present study aims to extend the investigation of native speaker mentoring programme on non-native English language teachers' professional development and identity construction in Malaysian context.

5 The case studies

The study discussed in this book adopted a multiple case study (Yin, 2009) approach within a qualitative interpretive research design. Case study was chosen as the methodology for this research as it offered a thick description of the context and provided in-depth insight into complicated situated and social issues involved in providing support for novice English as a Second Language (ESL) teachers during the *Native Speaker Programme*. Qualitative design allowed this study to explore the role that the programme plays in novice teachers' professional knowledge construction, practice, as well as identity formation through the voice of the practitioners who have experienced the programme. In addition, multiple cases in this study allow the researchers to provide interesting contrasts and corroboration across the cases.

Context of the study

The *Native Speaker Programme* can be considered as a combination of *sponsored professionalism* and *independent professionalism*. This is because while the programme requires the teacher to attend workshops, to be monitored and observed by their native English-speaking mentors and to be examined for their performance, the programme also encourages teachers to engage in reflective examination of their practice. Furthermore, the programme also promotes authentic and individual learning as well as learning through experience among the participating ESL teachers.

This programme was one of the initiatives taken by the Ministry of Education to enhance the English language mastery and improve the teaching and learning strategy of local English teachers in primary schools in Malaysia. In the programme, the native English-speaking mentors assisted participating teachers to improve their quality of teaching through activities such as Teacher Professional Development

(TPD) workshop, observation of teachers' classroom teaching and learning activities, interaction and discussion, collaboration with colleagues as well as co-teaching. In this mentoring programme, participating ESL teachers received 75 hours of professional input through individual mentoring at least once a fortnight as well as in situ mentoring and training.

The native English-speaking mentors would visit the participants twice a week in their schools to observe teachers' teaching and learning activities. The observation centres on teachers' effective use of teaching-learning resources, level and quality of pupil engagement in a lesson, and teachers' assessment and evaluation technique. In addition, native English-speaking mentors provided teachers with feedback on how to enhance the quality of teaching besides facilitating the teachers' teaching, learning activities through pair teaching, team-teaching, and demo teaching. In pair teaching, the mentor would teach alongside one mentee. On the other hand, in team-teaching, the mentor would teach together with all of the mentees from the same school. As for demo teaching, the mentor would demonstrate teaching and learning activities with the mentees sitting at the back of the class to observe the mentor's lesson. At the end of the year, the participating novice ESL teachers are expected to show improvement in the quality of their classroom teaching and learning. The participating novice teachers were also expected to exhibit improvement in their English language proficiency and to develop a reasonable amount of quality and suitable English teaching resources at the end of the year.

Furnished imagination

Drawing on a recent construct by Kiely and Askham (2012), *Furnished Imagination*, this section starts by laying out the theoretical dimensions of this study. Kiely and Askham (2012, p. 509) suggest that the understanding of ESL teachers' professional development can best be understood through the construct of *Furnished Imagination*, which is "an understanding of key elements of the knowledge bases, procedural competence in planning for and managing lessons, a disposition characterised by enthusiasm and readiness, and teacher identity: a sense of belonging in the world of TESOL". *Furnished Imagination* operates as a way to understand the impact of TESOL (Teaching English to Speakers of Other Languages) teacher learning during an early training context on their readiness for work. Kiely and Askham (2012) stressed that although it is unlikely for initial teacher development programme to transform novice ESL teachers into TESOL experts, it facilitates them to progress into a 'state of readiness' to start their teaching career and to continually engage in lifelong learning along the way. The term *imagination* in Kiely and Ashkam's recent construct represents a constructivist interpretation about knowledge. In this context, learning takes place through social interaction between novice ESL teachers with their mentors and peers during the mentoring programme to become a member of TESOL community. During this process, novice ESL teachers bring together the input that they gained during interactions with their self-image and their belief in their potential in forming their identity as a member of TESOL community. Hence, in the *Furnished Imagination* construct, "identity is future oriented, drawing on the capacity to imagine a transformed self and to see it as part of the narrative of personal history" (Kiely & Askham, 2012, p. 498).

It is important to note that identity formation does not merely rely on novice ESL teachers' sense of self-belief; instead, it includes teacher learning. To define learning, Kiely and Askham adopted Wenger's (1998) characteristics of learning that include *meaning, practice,* and *community.* Thus, the evidence on novice ESL teacher learning can be elicited through *meaning* – when the novice ESL teachers inform about their improvement in capacity, *practice* – when the novice ESL teachers explain and demonstrate the mutual practice within TESOL community, and *community* – when the novice ESL teachers identify themselves as one of the members of TESOL community through significant initiatives taken to develop their competency.

Furnished Imagination is a combination of knowledge, procedural awareness and skills, dispositions and identity that novice ESL teachers take from an initial teacher development as a readiness for work in TESOL. Therefore, the impact on ESL teacher professional development during an early training context on their readiness for work is deciphered through the expansion of their knowledge base, competency pertaining to teaching and learning procedures, motivated disposition, and TESOL teacher identity. The fusion of knowledge, procedural awareness and skills, dispositions and identity serves as a way of understanding how teachers construct their professional knowledge, as a way of tracking their professional practice, and as a way of capturing their professional identity formation.

The four novice ESL teachers

This study explored four novice ESL teachers' teaching experience to obtain a deep understanding of their learning experience, and to glean a detailed and holistic picture of the roles of the *Native Speaker*

Programme on novice ESL teachers' identity formation, personal practical knowledge construction, as well as practice. Two male and two female novice ESL teachers participated in this study. The selection of the four novice ESL primary school teachers was based on purposeful sampling. According to Merriam (1998), the assumption of what a researcher wants to discover, understand, and gain forms the foundation of purposeful sampling. Therefore, the researcher chose a sample from which "the most can be learned" (Merriam, 1998, p. 61).

In this study, the case is bounded by the fact that only novice ESL primary school teachers took part in the study and these teachers participated as mentees in the *Native Speaker Programme*. The criterion of a maximum of three years of teaching experience was also adopted. Before the beginning of the data collection, consent forms were given to the selected participants. The participants were also informed of their right to withdraw from participating in this research at any time during the conduct of this research. The participants were also briefed on the research purposes, research procedure, the expected amount and level of involvement from them, and the implication of this research on them prior to the data collection. For the purpose of writing the research findings, the real names of the participants were not revealed. Instead, they were given pseudonyms, namely Farhan, Nadya, Hafiz, and Suzanna.

Farhan

Farhan is a 27-year-old English teacher in a rural primary school in one of the states in the southern region of Malaysia. He received his bachelor's degree in education (Teaching English as a Second Language) from a public university in Malaysia. His first language is Malay, and he had two and a half years of experience in teaching English to primary school pupils. He was first posted to a rural primary school in a remote area in East Malaysia where he taught English to Year 4, Year 5, and Year 6 students. Due to adversities that he experienced as a new teacher in a rural school with limited facilities, he described his first year of teaching as 'not so much on teaching, but more on surviving'.

One year after his first posting, he was transferred to his current school that is situated in his own hometown. The school is located in a rural area of FELDA (Federal Land Development Authority) settlement, and most of his students are children and grandchildren of FELDA settlers, working in oil palm and rubber plantations. In the current school, he taught English to Year 1 and Year 5 students. As a Year 1 English teacher who is involved with the implementation of the new curriculum, KSSR (Primary School Standard Curriculum), he is required to participate as one of the mentees in the *Native Speaker Programme*.

His mentor, Sally is an English native speaker from the United Kingdom and has an extensive experience in teaching English language and training English language teachers in EFL countries like Japan, Thailand, and South Korea. She visited Farhan at his school two to four times per month to carry out mentoring activities such as observation and team-teaching. Sally also mentored other two English teachers in Farhan's school as well as few other English teachers in another two schools. Farhan described Sally as 'very helpful and cooperative' mentor.

As part of the mentoring programme, Farhan was required to attend the TPD workshops once a month. In the three-hour TPD workshop, which was organized by Sally and two other native speaker mentors, Farhan took part in various activities together with 35 other English teachers from different schools in the same district. The activities in the TPD workshop included lectures, microteaching, demonstration, presentation, group discussion, and quizzes.

Nadya

Nadya is an English language teacher in her mid-20s, teaching in a suburban primary school in one of the states in the central region of Malaysia. Her first language is Malay, and she holds a bachelor's degree in Teaching English as a Second Language (TESL) for Primary Education from a public university in Malaysia. Nadya admitted that teaching was her 'last choice of profession' and she was pressured by her father to enrol into the teacher education programme and subsequently to take up teaching as her career. As a novice teacher, she considered teaching English as an uninteresting job and she stated that being in the teacher education programme for four years did not change her negative perception towards the profession.

Nadya's first teaching position was at a rural primary school in one of the East Coast states of Malaysia, where she taught English to lower primary pupils. Since it was also the first year of the implementation of the new curriculum KSSR (Primary School Standard Curriculum), Nadya considered her first year of teaching as full of struggles and confusion as she felt lost with the newly implemented curriculum. Additionally, she faced difficulties in teaching English language to her indigenous pupils since she was not exposed to any input in dealing with indigenous pupils during her teacher education years.

Few months later, she moved to the current school to be near her family. In this suburban school, Nadya taught English to Year 1, Year 2, and Year 3 low-proficiency students. Although the school was located in a suburban area, most of the students came from low social economic status background where their parents working as farmers in farms nearby the school. Some of her students would rush home to help their parents in the farms after school.

As a Year 1 English teacher who must implement the newly introduced KSSR curriculum, she was selected to be a participant of the *Native Speaker Programme*. Nadya was first assigned Mark, a native speaker in his mid-30s from Canada as her mentor. However, two weeks later, Victoria replaced Mark as her new native speaker mentor. Victoria is in her late 40s who was born in the Philippines. Her first language is English, and she spent few years of her childhood in the United States. Victoria spoke English fluently with a hint of Filipino accent. She had an extensive experience as an ESL teacher teaching in private schools and universities in countries like the United States, Australia, and the United Kingdom.

As Nadya's mentor, Victoria would conduct classroom observation twice per month. As part of her mentor duties, Victoria would also carry out pair teaching where she would co-teach with Nadya, team-teaching with Nadya and her other mentees in the school, and demo teaching where she would demonstrate teaching and learning activities to her mentees. Furthermore, Victoria conducted TPD workshops once a month for all of her 23 mentees. As a participant of the *Native Speaker Programme*, Nadya was required to attend the TPD workshops. In the three hours of each TPD workshop, Nadya and other English teachers from different schools would take part in various learning activities such as lectures, group work, games, presentation, discussion, and quizzes.

Hafiz

Hafiz is a 25-year-old English teacher in a rural primary school located in the southern region of Malaysia. His first language is Malay, and he graduated with a first-class bachelor's degree in TESL from a local university in Malaysia. He started his teaching position at his current school right after he completed his teacher education and he had only been teaching for six months. His school was located in an agricultural area where most of the students came from families of farmers and labourers. On Hafiz's second day of work, his headmistress informed him that he was required to participate in the *Native Speaker*

Programme. Having a TESL background, the headmistress of the school placed a great emphasis on pupils' achievement in the English language. Hence, English teachers of the school were given the privilege to conduct all of their English lessons in a special air-conditioned room equipped with facilities called the English language centre (ELC). Most of the English lessons were conducted at the centre.

As a participant in the *Native Speaker Programme*, Hafiz worked with his native speaker mentor, Nate, who is in his late 20s. Although Nate has a master's degree in education, he had limited experience in ESL teaching context. He visits Farhan once a week on Thursday for an hour to carry out his mentoring duties such as tutorial, grammar quizzes, discussion, and observation. Nate was also mentoring other two English teachers in Hafiz's school as well as few other English teachers in other schools. Hafiz described Nate as a 'professional yet approachable' mentor.

Like other participants in the mentoring programme, Hafiz was required to attend TPD workshops once a month. In the TPD workshops, which were organized by Nate and two other native speaker mentors, Hafiz took part in various activities together with 60 other English teachers from different clusters and different schools in the same district. The activities in the TPD workshop included lectures, microteaching, demonstration, presentation, group discussion, and quizzes.

Moreover, as a participant in the programme, Hafiz was given the opportunity to take part as a presenter in a series of conferences called 'Best Practices', which was conducted by the Brighton Education Group. In the Best Practices Conferences, selected participants of the *Native Speaker Programme* presented and shared teaching methods that their mentors considered to be effective with teachers from other districts and states.

Suzanna

Suzanna is an English language teacher in her mid-20s. She teaches in a primary school in one of the states in the central region of Malaysia. Suzanna's first language is Malay, and she has a bachelor's degree in TESL from a public university in Malaysia. She started teaching at her current school right after she completed her teacher education in October 2010. At the time this study was carried out in 2013, Suzanna was in her third year of teaching. Suzanna was teaching English to Year 1 and Year 2 low-proficiency pupils.

Suzanna's school was located in a fishermen village. It was a rural school with approximately 300 students. Most of the students came from low socio-economic background where their parents work as fishermen, farmers, and labourers. As a lower primary English teacher, Suzanna was involved with the implementation of the new curriculum, KSSR (Primary School Standard Curriculum). Thus, she was required to participate in the *Native Speaker Programme*. As a participant of the programme, Suzanna informed that she needed to undergo about 75 hours of face-to-face interaction with her mentor through classroom observation and discussion of 10 lessons, peer teaching, and TPD workshops. In addition, she was required to produce suitable resources in print or in electronic forms.

In her first two years of participating in the programme, Suzanna was assigned Stella as her native speaker mentor. Stella, in her mid-40s, is an Australian. She had extensive experience teaching English as a second language to primary school students from China, Japan, and Korea back in her home country in Australia. Suzanna regarded Stella as a resourceful and skilful mentor due to her wide experience in ESL context. In addition, Suzanna described Stella as a 'traditional' person who loved telling her mentees stories about her family in Australia. Unfortunately, Stella decided to resign from her job as a mentor and returned to her family in Australia due to personal matters.

Stella's post was immediately replaced by John. In his mid-40s, John had enjoyed a long career with a non-governmental organization in the United States before he moved to Malaysia along with his wife who was also offered the job as native speaker mentor. Although, he did not have any experience in ESL teaching and learning, Suzanna considered John to be a good mentor who was committed to his job. Suzanna described John as a 'relaxed' but 'systematic' person, as he is always well prepared in each of his TPD workshops.

Data collection and analysis

To enhance the credibility of the findings and interpretations of this study, a variety of data sources as a means of triangulation (Merriam, 1998) were employed. Three data collection techniques were used in this qualitative multiple case study design (Yin, 2009): (a) in-depth interviews, (b) observations, and (c) personal document analysis.

In-depth interviews were used in this study to encourage the participants to describe and evaluate their own learning experiences thoroughly from their own perspectives. All the interviews were conducted face-to-face in the participants' school or at a place of their choice using an interview protocol that was developed based on relevant literature. The interviews were audiotaped for transcription purposes and transcribed immediately. Then, the researchers reviewed each transcription with written notes from the interview while listening to the corresponding tape.

Two types of observations were carried out for this study. Apart from observing the interactions between native English-speaking mentors and the participating novice ESL teacher during their TPD workshops, the researchers conducted classroom observations on novice ESL teachers' teaching and learning activities. As non-participating observers, these observations allowed the researchers to examine the mentoring activities during TPD workshops as well as the novice teachers' practice as ESL primary school teachers. To generate a thick description of the findings, the data were recorded using an audio recorder and field notes were written. Then, the researchers reviewed the recorded audios of observations with the field notes taken during the observations.

Documents are a constructive source of information, which provide data that are objective and unobtrusive (Creswell, 2011). In the present study, documents such as participants' lesson notes, circulars, lesson plans, records, and materials that they develop or receive during the programme and other potentially useful documents were collected with their permission. These collected documents provided the researcher with greater access in examining ways in which the *Native Speaker Programme* influences the novice ESL teachers' knowledge, practice, and identity and were used to supplement data from the interviews and observations.

Data collection and analysis occurred concurrently during the research. The data collection was completed within one-year period where data saturation was achieved as a prolonged engagement to ensure trustworthiness. In this study, inductive data analysis approach (Mackey & Gass, 2005) was employed in generating categories, themes, and pattern. To synthesize the data, major patterns or themes that are linked together, either similarly or differently, that collectively describe or analyse the novice ESL teachers' learning experience were identified. Then, patterns were compared and contrasted within categories and this was followed by patterns across categories. Finally, the researchers situate the findings within the existing body of literature on teacher learning and professional development, and juxtapose them with issues that have been discussed in previous research on novice ESL teacher learning.

6 Enhancing professional knowledge through mentoring

This chapter explores the influence of a mentoring programme, the *Native Speaker Programme*, on four novice ESL teachers' professional knowledge in their beginning years of teaching. *Furnished Imagination* was used as the theoretical underpinning of this study because it allows the present study to highlight what the novice teachers have learnt during the *Native Speaker Programme*, how this learning was established in the programme and resumed in the classroom. The participants, in this case the novice ESL teachers – Farhan, Nadya, Hafiz, and Suzanna – construct their professional knowledge by combining their sense of self and their sense of possibility with input gained from the *Native Speaker Programme* which involved Teachers Professional Development (TPD) workshops, classroom observations, co-teaching, and discussion with their native speaker mentors as well as collaboration with peers.

Bridging the gap between teacher education programmes and the real classroom

The case studies presented in this chapter revealed that the *Native Speaker Programme* contributed to novice teachers' professional knowledge construction by bridging the gap between their teacher education training and real classroom. For all the participants, the programme seemed to bridge the gap between their teacher education training and real classroom through different ways. For Farhan, his participation in the programme enabled him to revisit the knowledge that he had learnt during his teacher education programme. In contrast, Nadya believed that the mentoring programme provided her with practical input that was readily available to be employed into her lessons. Nadya considered the practical input presented in the mentoring programme supplemented her existing theoretical knowledge that she gained during teacher education programme. On the other hand,

Hafiz considered the programme complemented his existing knowledge that he gained during teacher education programme with additional knowledge and skills. As for Suzanna, the programme helped her to reinforce prior knowledge that she acquired during teacher education programme with new knowledge.

Revisiting knowledge

Farhan viewed the *Native Speaker Programme* as "a programme to reinforce what we have learned, to refresh my knowledge, skills and memories". Through mentoring activities and the TPD workshops, the programme enables him to recall knowledge and skills that he had previously acquired. As to the structure of curriculum in the teacher education programme that emphasized more on theory rather than practice, it was challenging him to sustain his knowledge and skills since he had limited opportunity to experience the authentic classroom environment in schools as an English teacher. The *Native Speaker Programme* allowed him to engage in more hands-on activity where he could directly employ his existing knowledge and skills with the help from his mentor in his classroom.

Theory versus practical

In Nadya's case, the *Native Speaker Programme* facilitated her professional knowledge construction by bridging the gap between her teacher education programs at university with the real classroom. Nadya's juxtaposition on the knowledge that she learnt during teacher education programme with the knowledge that she gained through the *Native Speaker Programme* made her realize that the knowledge she learnt at the university was mostly theoretical. In contrast, the knowledge that she gained through the programme was practical and readily to be employed into teaching and learning activities in her classroom.

With her mentor, Victoria's presence in Nadya's classroom during school visits allowed her to receive relevant and constructive feedback on improving her lessons as the feedback given by Victoria was based on her critical analysis on the situation in Nadya's classroom. Nadya shared her view on how she could use the knowledge on classroom management that she gained from her mentor as a hands-on input, although she had learnt about it earlier during her studies.

> Personally as an ESL teacher, most of the input given in the programme was already given during my studies, so for me, the most

valuable input that she (Victoria) gave me is classroom management. So it helps me managing my class because she will be there, she looks at the situation, she evaluates the situation and she gives suggestion.

This hands-on input knowledge not only contributed to Nadya's professional knowledge construction, but also allowed her to improve her professional practice and to form her professional identity.

Complementing the existing knowledge

As for Hafiz, knowledge and skills presented in the programme complemented his existing knowledge gained during teacher education programme in the university. Hafiz realized that although certain knowledge presented by his mentor was not new to him, he had learnt them during the teacher education programme at the university; he found that the knowledge presented in the programme was more comprehensive and tailored to meet the needs of the pupils in a real classroom. To substantiate his realization, Hafiz drew an example from the use of hot seating, a drama activity for teaching English. As a fresh graduate, he still remembered that he learnt the techniques of teaching English using drama back at the university. However, he considered what he had learnt during the teacher education programme as just an introduction to the technique as he did not have the opportunity to apply them in a real classroom situation. On the other hand, now that he is an ESL teacher, he is able to relearn the technique extensively through the programme by applying his knowledge on drama activities suggested by his mentor into his lessons. Thus, the *Native Speaker Programme* extended his existing knowledge from the 'what' knowledge to the 'how' knowledge. Hafiz strongly felt that the additional knowledge that he acquired through the *Native Speaker Programme* enabled him to accelerate his professional development. When asked to imagine his life as a novice ESL teacher without the mentoring programme, Hafiz has the following to say:

We gain experience as we go along. The more we teach, the more we learn. However, with this programme, there's additional knowledge apart from learning through our own experience. So it makes my development as a teacher faster.

Reinforcing existing knowledge

Suzanna found that some of the input presented in the *Native Speaker Programme* expanded her existing knowledge that she gained from teacher education programme on certain area. Using the knowledge on teaching phonics for example, Suzanna asserted that her teacher education programme only provided her with knowledge about phonics. She claimed that the *Native Speaker Programme* extended her basic knowledge about phonics by providing her with additional input on how to teach phonics to pupils. The input on how to teach phonics presented by her mentors assisted Suzanna in conducting lessons on pronunciation with low-proficiency pupils. Moreover, teaching phonics was new to Suzanna as it was just recently introduced in the new KSSR (Kurikulum Standard Sekolah Rendah) curriculum. Hence, Suzanna felt that the input on phonics that she learned in the programme expanded her existing knowledge on the area, thus allowing her to conduct lesson on pronunciation confidently. She said,

> Although I have learnt about phonics in the university, I could barely recall. Nevertheless, through this programme, I also learn about the implementation part, the practical knowledge – how to teach phonics. I am now quite confident to teach phonics.

Expansion of knowledge base

Mentoring provides support for novice teachers to increase their knowledge base (Malderez, 2009; Reid, 2010; Vaught, 2010). This is because when new teachers maintained their role as learners who were willing to learn from their mentors, they were able to enhance their content knowledge as they benefit from their mentors' expertise. The findings from Reid's (2010) study suggested that mentoring programme reinforced new teachers' knowledge particularly on general pedagogical knowledge and pedagogical content knowledge. Correspondingly, the findings of the present study show similar results as all of the participants reported that the *Native Speaker Programme* contributed to their pedagogical content knowledge. In addition to pedagogical content knowledge, the findings indicated that mentoring facilitated ESL novice teachers in contributing to their knowledge about language, pupils' needs, context, and process knowledge.

Knowledge about language

The *Native Speaker Programme* facilitated Farhan's professional knowledge construction as it provided him with the platform to expand his knowledge base. One aspect of knowledge that Farhan realized has improved throughout the *Native Speaker Programme* was his knowledge about language (Bartels, 2009). Farhan points out that the programme provided him the opportunity to improve his English proficiency. Farhan believed that he needed to practice his English so that he would not 'lose it'. However, the school environment in which he was teaching did not permit him to maximize the use of English through communication due to the absence of the need to do so. Farhan's mentor provides him the opportunity to engage in authentic social conversation using English language. He felt "thankful for having a mentor because it is through her I can at least maintain my level of English". In fact, when asked on the most valuable aspect about working with his native speaker mentor, Farhan had the following to say:

> For me, the most valuable aspect is actually to have someone you can talk to in English and then, someone to check your speaking skill, because for me language is something that you have to practice. That's why I value her presence and the fact that we can at least communicate in English, to have a speaking partner and she can also check on my grammar, my use of language.

Likewise, for Suzanna, her participation in the *Native Speaker Programme* assisted her to improve her English-speaking skills. Just like the other participants, the programme provided her with a platform to exercise her speaking skills by engaging in authentic conversation with her native speaker mentor in a natural setting. Suzanna had the opportunity to use English freely without getting obtrusive comments on her mistake from her mentors. This encouraged Suzanna to maximize her interaction with her mentor, which enabled her to practice her speaking skills. Suzanna believed that through practice, she was able to improve her speaking skills. She said,

> As my mentor is a native speaker, it encourages me to speak English. You know my school doesn't provide English-speaking environment. So, when I speak English with John or Stella, it kind of improves my speaking skills... Although as English teachers, we are scared of making mistake, these mentors are very relaxed. So I felt encouraged. Free to talk.

Suzanna considered John and Stella's status as the native speaker of English language made them superior mentors as compared to non-native speaker mentors. She believed that as English native speakers, John and Stella have the credibility to provide her with accurate input on ESL teaching and learning. Hence, Suzanna felt fortunate that she has the opportunity to work closely with John and Stella. This was especially when she realized that not all English teachers in Malaysia were given the chance to improve themselves with the help of the native speakers of English.

Suzanna's belief on the superiority of the English native speaker status motivated her to participate seriously in the native speaker mentor. The expertise shown by both of her mentors, especially Stella, in suggesting and demonstrating teaching and learning activities that were effective for her low-proficiency pupils, supported Suzanna's belief about the native speakers' competence in providing her with accurate input. Suzanna presumed that it was Stella's extensive experience in teaching English to ESL pupils in Australia that contributed to her expertise as a mentor. Therefore, Suzanna's perception on the superiority of the English native speaker status encouraged her to maximize her learning in the *Native Speaker Programme* and this contributes to her professional knowledge construction as an ESL teacher.

As for Nadya, she realized that her grammatical knowledge has improved throughout her participation in the *Native Speaker Programme* as there is a great emphasis placed on grammar. In the TPD workshop observed by the researcher, Victoria carried out few sessions on teaching grammar to the participating teachers. This included lessons on parts of speech, subject-verb agreement, relative clause, modals, tenses, and wh-questions. Victoria used language games for teaching parts of speech to her mentees. In the activity, participating teachers were assigned into two teams. Each team was given a tambourine, and they were required to shake the tambourine in order to answer the questions. Teachers took turns to answer questions on identifying parts of speech of words in sentences read by Victoria. Teams were rewarded with points for every correct answer.

Similarly, for Hafiz, his mentor Nate conducted many sessions on grammar lesson during TPD workshops. In addition, to reinforce Hafiz's knowledge on presented grammar rules, his mentor carried out simple grammar quizzes during tutorial session when he visited Hafiz and his other mentees at school. Furthermore, the programme enhanced Hafiz's knowledge on pronunciation. As a non-native speaker of English language, Hafiz found it difficult to ensure the accuracy of his pronunciation when speaking English. This is because for Hafiz, unlike grammar, which could easily be learned by understanding its rules through books on his own, learning pronunciation required him to rely on native speakers so that he could listen to the correct articulation of the word and imitate the sound. Hence, having native speaker mentors enabled him to learn pronunciation effectively as it provided him the access to listen to native speakers' accurate pronunciation. Hafiz said,

> Maybe before this, we say this word in our own Malaysian way, but during the TPD, he (Nate) pronounces it differently, and we ask him, he said 'Oh, in UK it is like this'... so, we learn something new from that. We never realize we pronounce the word wrongly until during the TPD workshop. So when my mentor says certain words, only I realize my mistake.

As a native speaker mentor, Nate plays a significant role in contributing to Hafiz's knowledge about language. Hafiz viewed Nate as a good model of the English language for him and his colleagues. As a native speaker of English language, Hafiz believed that Nate had the credibility to model a correct use of English language. According to Hafiz, this was especially important in the learning of pronunciation, as he believed that he was able to learn pronunciation indirectly through modelling after his mentor's pronunciation. However, Hafiz admitted that sometimes there was uncertainty about the accurate way of pronouncing certain words, particularly during the TPD workshop when all the three mentors spoke with different accent. Three of them come from different countries; Nate is from the United Kingdom, while both Patrick and Deborah are from the United States with Deborah speaking with a hint of African-American slang. Nevertheless, Hafiz learned that it actually gave him the opportunity to learn more about the diversity of English language accent when Nate and the other two mentors enlightened him and other participating teachers about differences in pronouncing certain words between native speakers in the United Kingdom and in the United States. Hence, he took this opportunity to maximize the effort in improving his English language proficiency by communicating with Nate, his mentor.

Pedagogical Content Knowledge

In terms of pedagogical knowledge, Farhan believed that the *Native Speaker Programme* encouraged him to broaden his knowledge base on the teaching of pronunciation to primary school pupils. In Malaysia, the teaching of pronunciation is considered to be challenging by the ESL teachers due to their lack of knowledge on pronunciation content and instruction (Ahmad Shah, Othman, & Senom, 2017). This issue is confirmed by the current study as Farhan regarded the teaching of pronunciation as something that "we were not really exposed to" during his teacher education programme. Ironically, the teaching of pronunciation appeared to be the core syllabus in the new KSSR curriculum. Due to lack of knowledge on the teaching of pronunciation before his participation in the *Native Speaker Programme*, it was problematic for Farhan to carry out lesson on phonics to Year 1 pupils. Thus, Farhan valued his experience as a participant in the programme as he found it broadened his knowledge on teaching pronunciation to Year 1 pupils. He said,

> The biggest contribution of this programme is for the phonics that I have to teach to the Year 1. Because it is helpful.

The programme also assisted Nadya's professional knowledge construction by enhancing her pedagogic content knowledge. This is evident when Nadya shared her experience on learning how to cope with challenges in teaching young learners who were having difficulty in understanding abstract concept. According to Nadya, her mentor encouraged her to use gestures to explain meaning of words for her young learners. As for words that were unexplainable through nonverbal gestures, her mentor suggested that she translates the words into the first language in order to explain the meaning to her young learners.

> ...because the pupils are using English as a foreign language, so she said sometimes it is okay to translate to Bahasa but not too much, and she also taught us how to use nonverbal communication to give meaning to some words.

Nadya believed that the use of nonverbal gestures and first language in explaining meaning of words enabled her to maximize the effectiveness of her teaching and learning activities. When the pupils understood the meaning of main words emphasized in her lesson, they were able to pay more attention to the lesson, participate more actively in the activities, and ultimately experience a more enjoyable lesson.

In addition, the programme provided Nadya with the opportunity to broaden her knowledge base on classroom management. Although Nadya still appeared to be struggling with classroom management during the classroom observations carried out by the researcher, she admitted that her knowledge on classroom control has improved throughout the programme. Nadya received a lot of valuable input to improve her classroom management from her mentor through mentoring activities such as co-teaching, demo teaching, and classroom observation. During co-teaching and demo teaching conducted by her mentor, Victoria demonstrated effectual classroom control techniques that were suitable for Nadya's pupils. This, in turn, enabled Nadya to build better understanding on effective classroom control. Nadya also gained useful knowledge on classroom management from constructive feedback given by Victoria through classroom observations.

> When Victoria is visiting, she'll be entering all the classes we are teaching. So she will observe and sometimes she will give sugges-tions. She will give you ideas and basically, input for you to control your class.

Another aspect of pedagogical content knowledge highlighted in the programme was the development of teaching and learning resources. Hafiz found that his mentor demonstrated a strong commitment in facilitating Hafiz to develop resources that were suitable for his pupils. Nate played an important role in assisting him and his colleagues to set up the school's English Language Centre. According to Hafiz, Nate provided them with suggestions of resources to be included in the centre as well as helping them in selecting and finding appropriate resources for the centre. Since purchasing teaching resources would cost a for-tune, Hafiz and his colleagues developed most of the teaching aids such as pop-up books, thematic walls, charts, masks, puppets, reading cards, art and craft materials, and board games on their own. With the help and guidance from his mentor, Hafiz was able to transform a traditional classroom into an exciting English Language Centre that was rich with English language teaching and learning resources. On developing his own teaching resources, Hafiz explained,

> Because if you notice, in my ELC room, we have pop-up books and many other resources. We actually learn how to make pop up books. You know how expensive it is to purchase that pop-up books right? So we learnt to do that!

As a lower primary ESL teacher, Suzanna was required to use the new KSSR curriculum to carry out her English lesson. In the new syllabus, there were few new components such as phonetics and language arts that Suzanna needed to include in her lessons. Having little knowledge on effective ways to incorporate language arts component into her les-sons, Suzanna found that it was challenging to integrate the language arts component from the KSSR syllabus into her teaching and learn-ing activities. Nevertheless, Suzanna found the input from her mentor to be valuable in enhancing her understanding about the appropriate strategy in implementing language arts using the language content in the KSSR syllabus into her lesson. When asked about the most valuable aspect of knowledge that she has learnt from the programme, Suzanna answered,

> Language arts because it is a new component in the curriculum. So, usually we just simply use puppets, songs in the lesson. But, now, how to use and maximize it in the classroom, with the language content that we want to introduce to kids? So John taught us how to use puppets in the lessons. How to integrate songs in the lesson – the correct steps. Although it looks simple, actually it has certain steps in order for the pupils to gain the knowledge.

With valuable guidance and input from John, Suzanna was more confident in integrating the new component into teaching and learning activities for her low-proficiency pupils.

Curricular knowledge

Thirdly, the findings suggested the *Native Speaker Programme* contributed to novice teachers' professional knowledge by providing them with guidance from the expert. Each participant had different views of their mentors' expertise in facilitating them to enhance their knowledge in ESL teaching. Farhan viewed his mentors as facilitators and English-speaking partners, while Nadya considered her mentor as her source of reference who helped her to improve her knowledge throughout the programme. For Hafiz and Suzanna, they acknowledged their mentors' native speaker status and role as the agent of change that supported them to construct their professional knowledge as ESL teachers.

According to Farhan, the *Native Speaker Programme* played a significant role in contributing to his professional knowledge construction as it enabled him to receive guidance from the expert. Farhan believed that the most significant role of his native speaker mentor was as a facilitator for him to adjust himself with changes in his working environment. Since Farhan was assigned to teach English to Year 1 pupils, he was required to implement the new KSSR curriculum into his teaching and learning activities. Prior to his participation in the programme, Farhan experienced great difficulties to cope with major changes in the English language syllabus for Year 1 pupils. In one of the interviews, Farhan recollected his daunting experience in implementing KSSR before his participation in the *Native Speaker Programme*:

> I taught Year 1 for the first year of English KSSR curriculum implementation. So, during that time as a teacher, I think I was a bit clueless, a bit in the dark about how I am going to carry out the whole KSSR thing.

Fortunately, the programme enabled Farhan to cope with the new curriculum as his mentor, Sally assisted him by suggesting and demonstrating suitable teaching and learning activities through lesson planning and team-teaching. In the fifth interview, Farhan elucidated Sally's determination in facilitating him to conduct teaching and learning activities in accordance with the new syllabus:

> She really went through the new textbook and syllabus (KSSR) so that's why when she come and help us, we get adequate help and guidance for us to carry out our job in teaching English to young learners.

Likewise, Nadya felt that her mentor Victoria played an important role in contributing to her professional knowledge construction. Nadya viewed Victoria as her ultimate source of reference. This is because whenever she encountered problems related to teaching and learning activities, she would ask for Victoria's help. Nadya believed that her mentor's suggestions were the best solutions for her classroom problems as Victoria had adequate understanding and familiarity with her pupils and her school. In addition, Victoria had an extensive experience as an ESL teacher teaching in private schools and universities in the United States, Australia, and the United Kingdom. As such, Nadya always trusted her judgement. Having Victoria as her ultimate source of reference allowed Nadya to gain knowledge in the most effective ways to cater to students' differences during teaching and learning activities. In addition, Nadya would always consult Victoria if she has questions on English language. She believed that as a native speaker of English language, Victoria's answers to her questions on English language were 'accurate'. In addition, Victoria's willingness to guide her in improving her English language encouraged her to learn more about the language.

> If I am having trouble, I have someone to go to. By having my mentor, I can ask her things regarding teaching and the language

especially. It is very good. It is like having a living dictionary. And a living grammar book.

Nadya's mentor also assisted her to cope with changes in her work environment. As a lower primary English teacher, Nadya was entrusted to carry out a newly implemented LINUS (Literacy and Numeracy Screening) Programme for her pupils. LINUS is an intervention programme, which aims to promote equality in education for lower primary school pupils – Year 1 to Year 3. Pupils were required to undergo screening test at the early stage of schooling so that teachers were able to identify their strengths and weaknesses in literacy and numeracy skills. Subsequently, weaker pupils will be given extra attention and assistance so that they will be able to keep up in mainstream classes. Since LINUS programme required Nadya to employ different materials, techniques, and approaches than what she normally used for her lesson to prepare the lower proficiency pupils for the screening test, Nadya found herself struggling in implementing LINUS programme. As a mentor, Victoria assisted Nadya in coping with the newly implemented programme by providing her with necessary input that she requested from the District Education Office. Nadya explained that

> Now, we have LINUS for English, our mentor helps us to understand and also to deliver this LINUS programme inside the classroom. If we did not understand anything or if we are having difficulties, she will go to the PPD (District Education Office) and say – my mentees are having problem with this LINUS programme. So how can I help them? So she did that and came back presenting to us a PowerPoint presentation, with all those teaching aids and things you can use to deliver the LINUS programme.

In order to assist Nadya to execute the LINUS programme, Victoria taught her to prepare suitable teacher resources and teaching activities for her weaker pupils to enable them to exit the LINUS class and join the mainstream class.

As a novice ESL teacher with just one year of teaching experience, Nadya felt that the programme provided necessary support and assistance for her to carry out her duties. When asked on the role of the programme in helping her to cope with the challenges that she faced as a novice teacher, Nadya had the following to say:

> It is like... a cane for you to hold on. When you are falling down, you have something to hold on. That is what I considered the

programme is. When you are having trouble, you have someone to ask. And you have someone to refer to – that is what the programme is to me.

In Suzanna's case, her mentor was seen as someone who facilitated her journey into the teaching community. As a novice teacher, Suzanna felt a little lost when she first started teaching at her current school. Like the others, she faced difficulty in implementing the new curriculum in her classroom. In order to enable Suzanna to cope with the new curriculum, her mentors provided her with valuable knowledge and skills on phonics and language arts component during the TPD workshops. Stella and John would also make sure that the input given was relevant to her situation by asking Suzanna about the teaching aspect that she wanted assistance. In addition, her mentors would demonstrate the teaching and learning activities on phonic and language arts through peer teaching, so that Suzanna had a good understanding on how to carry out lessons on those new components. In this context, her mentors took the role as agents of change who facilitated Suzanna to cope with new changes in the curriculum. She explained,

> In coping with changes, the major things that they have taught were phonics and language arts. During the peer teaching, I will personally ask my mentors, please demonstrate this phonics activity; I need to see before I can do it on my own. They would demonstrate, and from there, I learnt how they carry out the activities.

The programme also contributed to Suzanna's professional knowledge construction by providing her hands-on inputs that were applicable to her classroom. This is because all of the knowledge and skills presented by her mentors were aligned with the new KSSR curriculum and suitable for her low-proficiency pupils. In addition, her mentors would use the prescribed KSSR textbook as their main reference in suggesting teaching and learning activities. This helped Suzanna in navigating the new KSSR curriculum and felt confident in her instructional practices. She explained,

> The mentors would focus on KSSR. No matter what activities they introduce, they must be based on the KSSR and textbook. So, I feel I am on the right track.

In addition, Suzanna's learning process was reinforced through the observation of her teaching and learning activities by her mentor.

According to Suzanna, her mentors observed over 30 lessons throughout the three years of her participation in the programme. After each observation, her mentors would give her constructive feedback on her lessons. Suzanna regarded the feedback given to her as valuable because it allowed her to have a better understanding of good teaching practices and contributed to her professional knowledge as an ESL teacher.

Social and contextual dimensions

Lastly, the findings from the current study implied that the *Native Speaker Programme* contributed to novice teachers' professional development by providing them the opportunity to engage in enriching learning activities. All of the participants recognized the positive qualities of the learning activities offered by the programme. Two of the participants, Nadya and Hafiz, held similar view that the programme acts as a platform that promotes exchange of ideas. As for Suzanna, she believed that the programme contributed to her professional knowledge construction through peer teaching that assisted her to sharpen her knowledge and skills.

From Nadya's point of view, the *Native Speaker Programme* assisted her professional knowledge construction by providing her the platform to exchange of ideas with other participating teachers. She maintained that the activities in the programme promoted cooperation and teamwork among her peers. This is evident when Nadya talked about sharing teaching materials and lesson plans with her colleagues from different schools.

> We share things among participating teachers, like teaching ideas. So we compile everything and share it using Dropbox so everyone can use the same materials and the same handouts or ideas in their classroom. For example, I have Alphabots video clip so I share with them in the dropbox. Some teachers may not know where to find the video, so when I share, they can use it.

Through the exchange of ideas during the programme, Nadya was able to attain useful insights from her colleagues on different techniques of teaching and learning activities. Moreover, the exchange of ideas enabled participating teachers to minimize their workload in preparing materials for lessons, as they were able to incorporate suitable materials and lesson plans from their colleagues into their own classroom.

Similarly, for Hafiz, the *Native Speaker Programme* assisted his professional knowledge construction through enriching learning activities. For instance, the TPD workshops provided many opportunities for Hafiz and other participants to share teaching ideas and activities. According to Hafiz, other participating teachers understood the challenges that he faced as a new ESL teacher. They were aware of the difficulties in teaching English to low-proficiency pupils in the rural area. Hence, Hafiz was able to benefit from the interaction with his peers particularly in learning new teaching and learning techniques that were effective and suitable for his pupils. He explained,

> Most of the time, when we go to TPD session, they will group us. So we will be in groups that involve teachers from different school, so in a way, we mingle. Let say, they ask us to do certain activities, and then we have to present the activities, so we work together. So there are exchanges of ideas, sharing. I think it is good. At least we learn from other people who hold the same position with us. So they know the challenges.

In addition, Hafiz had the opportunity to attend the Best Practices Conferences, which enabled him to enhance his knowledge particularly in English teaching techniques and activities. According to Hafiz, participating in such conference was a new learning experience for him. He found that being able to learn from other teachers from different districts as a rejuvenating and enjoyable learning experience. He discovered that he gained new insight pertaining to teaching ideas through the knowledge presented by participants in the parallel sessions at the conference.

In Suzanna's case, she found the peer teaching activity very enriching. Suzanna and her mentors would plan their lesson together prior to the actual class. Based on the learning objectives, they discussed and selected suitable activities that they can use for Suzanna's low-proficiency learners. Then, they prepared necessary teaching materials for that lesson and delegated lesson slots among themselves. According to Suzanna, she would request her mentors to carry out activities that were unfamiliar to her. During the actual class, both Suzanna and her mentors, John or Stella, would take turns in conducting the lesson. Although Suzanna were initially sceptical about the feasibility of certain activities, John and Stella's success in conducting the lesson proved that the suggested activities were indeed possible to be carried out for her low-proficiency pupils. Moreover, through the demonstration of activities shown by her mentors during peer teaching, Suzanna was able to learn the right ways to conduct those activities. This provided Suzanna with better understanding on effective teaching techniques for her low-proficiency pupils. This, in turn, contributed to Suzanna's professional knowledge construction as an ESL teacher.

In conclusion, the study found that the programme contributed to the novice ESL teachers' professional knowledge by bridging the gap between their teacher education training and real classroom, expanding their knowledge base, curriculum knowledge, and contextual dimensions.

7 Professional practice development through mentoring

This chapter discusses how a mentoring programme, the *Native Speaker Programme*, contributes to novice ESL teachers' professional practice. The case studies are presented through a discussion on how the mentoring programme influenced the novice teachers' professional practice as ESL primary school teachers in their situated sociocultural context. In the mentoring programme, the novice teachers' professional practices were enhanced through their participation and interaction in the community of English teachers participating in the programme. The findings revealed that the programme contributed to novice ESL teachers' professional practice in terms of (a) classroom management, (b) teaching and learning, and (c) reflective practice.

Enhancing classroom management

Novice teachers face many challenges as they learn how to teach in their first year (Farrell, 2008). One of the challenges is classroom management. The findings of this study indicated that the mentoring programme allowed novice ESL teachers to enhance their professional practice in terms of their classroom management. Through the mentoring programme, the novice teachers learnt about the nature of establishing and maintaining classroom control. They also acquired a few classroom routines and tried them out with their mentors' support.

Attention grabber

For Hafiz, classroom management was one aspect of teaching that he admitted to be the most challenging. During all the observations made on Hafiz's classroom teaching and learning activities, he seemed to be struggling with his classroom control. In his first classroom observation, Hafiz seemed to be having some problems in delivering simple and effective classroom instructions while conducting teaching and learning activities with his mixed-ability pupils. Hafiz had the tendency to use long and confusing instructions with a monotonous tone of voice. As a result, his pupils seemed confused with the task assigned to them and they started to talk to each other and make a lot of noise.

Apart from that, the researcher noted that Hafiz's classroom management problem was caused by his lack of thoughtfulness in selecting suitable activities to cater to his mixed-ability pupils. During three classroom observations conducted by the researcher, Hafiz was seen to assign similar tasks to all pupils despite their differences in language ability. While Hafiz was assisting the low-proficiency pupils in completing the assigned tasks, the more proficient pupils who had completed the assigned tasks were left with no tasks to complete. This led them to engage in small talks and disturbing their friends.

With the help from his mentor, Hafiz improved on his instructional practices as an ESL teacher as he was provided with guidance in improving his classroom management skills. Hafiz points out that one of the classroom management techniques that he learnt from his mentor, Nate, was attention grabber. Prior to his participation in the programme, Hafiz often resorted to ineffective methods such as yelling and nagging to his pupils, asking them to be quiet in order to keep the class under control. However, after Hafiz learnt to use the attention grabber technique to capture his pupils' attention into his lessons, he no longer employs those ineffective methods to control his class.

The effectiveness of attention grabber technique as suggested by Hafiz's mentor was evident throughout the classroom observations conducted by the researcher. Whenever the pupils started to make noise, Hafiz would recapture their attention into his lesson by saying the phrase 'Eyes on me!' loudly. All the pupils then immediately replied by saying the phrase 'Eyes on you!' loudly, and they began to pay their attention to Hafiz. Other than that, he would call out the name of the class that he was teaching out loud, for example '2 Bestari!' and similarly, the pupils would immediately reply the phrase 'Aye! Aye! Captain!' and refocused their attention to his lesson.

While Hafiz admitted that his participation in the programme contributed to some improvement of his classroom management skills, he expected more input and guidance from his mentor on classroom management skills. Hafiz often asked for Nate's suggestion on suitable classroom management techniques for his pupils. However, due to time constraints and other commitment, Nate did not manage to provide personalized techniques that were suitable for Hafiz's pupils. Hafiz felt that the TPD workshops focused more on teaching and learning activities rather than input on classroom management. He believed that input on classroom management should be given more emphasis in the mentoring programme to help struggling novice teachers.

Rules establishment

As for Farhan, one of the helpful classroom management techniques that he learnt from his mentor was the rules establishment that formed at the beginning of school session each year. He admitted that in the previous year, he had poor classroom control when he was first assigned as a class teacher for Year 1 pupils. Nevertheless, he realized that it was important for him to establish a set of rules and 'get connected' with the pupils to identify their learning preferences at the beginning of the year to ensure the teaching and learning activities could be conducted smoothly. Hence, the following year, he decided to use the suggested techniques by his mentor and it appeared to be effective as he had a good control of his classroom and better classroom management. He said,

> So, during the first year, I was quite strict with the children. But nowadays, no more because, you can also manage the children or make them listen to you without being strict...

Clear instruction

In Suzanna's case, her mentors seemed to have a positive impact on her classroom practices as they provided her guidance in improving her classroom management. Through the demonstration of classroom management skills and techniques by her mentors during peer teaching, Suzanna realized that clear instruction played an important role in maintaining classroom control. Just like other novice teachers, Suzanna faced classroom management challenges during her first year of teaching. For Suzanna, classroom management was even more challenging when she was assigned a larger class with 36 pupils as compared to those with just 20–25 pupils. Suzanna found her first year of teaching as quite challenging since she has not established her "teaching style and classroom rules are still on trial and error". However, through the mentoring programme, she was able to recognize the importance of giving clear instructions during teaching and learning activities as demonstrated by her mentors.

According to Suzanna, her first mentor, Stella, had a very formal and systematic way for classroom management. Stella would explain to the pupils the rules that she wanted them to adhere to. In addition, she made word cards with phrases such as 'listen to me', 'point', and 'please be seated', and used them to control the class during team-teaching. Whenever she encountered any misbehaviour, she simply reminded the pupils about the rules that she had established without raising her voice. Moreover, Stella gave clear instructions on activities by using simple words and actions as well as by demonstrating the activities to the pupils. From Suzanna's observation of Stella's classroom management techniques during peer teaching, she learnt to give clear instructions while carrying out the teaching and learning activities.

Cooperative learning

Another classroom management strategy, which Suzanna learnt from the programme, is the use of cooperative learning activities. At the beginning of her career as an ESL teacher, Suzanna often found it difficult to find activities to accommodate her learners' different levels of language proficiency. It is common that the more capable pupils would complete the task assigned faster than the less able ones. Thus, when the more capable pupils were left with nothing to do, they ended up chatting and distracting other pupils who have not completed their tasks. In order to prevent this problem, her mentor, John, suggested that she employ cooperative learning activities in her lessons.

In one of the observations of Suzanna's lesson, she was seen to conduct pronunciation tasks where the pupils were instructed to work together in order to complete the task. The more capable pupils were entrusted with more complex task to assist their peers in completing the activities, keeping them fully occupied and leaving them with no time to misbehave. Furthermore, Suzanna discovered that cooperative learning activities could facilitate her pupils' learning, as some of the pupils were more comfortable to learn from their peers than from the teacher. Therefore, through the guidance given by her mentor, Suzanna was able to improve her instructional practices by employing cooperative learning activities into her lesson. Suzanna points out,

> John taught us for mixed ability class, ask the pupils who have completed their task earlier to teach their friends. Yes, he demonstrated that during peer teaching. Call one student who has finished the task and ask him to help his friends to complete the task.

Discrepancy between mentor's guidance and classroom practices

In contrast to the other participants in this study, Nadya's classroom practices were not congruent with her knowledge on the ideal practice gained from the programme and her actual practices in the classroom. During the third interview, Nadya admitted that at the beginning of the year, she used to bring a cane into her classroom with the hope that it would help her with classroom control. Nadya asserted that her mentor has helped her to adjust her classroom management style from threat to deal with misbehaviour with a more appropriate approach. As an alternative to using the cane for classroom control, Nadya was advised to employ a more humanistic approach by her mentor. However, during the second classroom observation, Nadya was seen to continue bringing the cane into her classroom. Furthermore, Nadya was observed by the researcher to strike the cane loudly on the table whenever the pupils started to make noise. This contradicted with her mentor's suggestion, which was to use the humanistic approach for classroom control. In fact, there was no evidence of any changes in Nadya's way of dealing with misbehaviours during all the three observations of her lessons in her classroom.

After her second classroom observation, Nadya told the researcher that she was actually still struggling with classroom management. She felt that the use of cane was more effective and 'easy' as compared to using the humanistic approach for classroom control particularly with large class of 40 pupils like hers. In addition, she also expressed her frustration with her school superiors for allocating too many pupils in a class. While teaching a large class of high-proficiency pupils was manageable for Nadya, teaching a low-proficiency class with too many pupils was very challenging for her as a novice teacher. Although she had voiced her concern over this matter to the school superiors, she felt that her school could not resolve the problem due to limited resources.

Borg (2009) asserts that teachers should not be blamed for the discrepancy between their ideals and their actual practice as they face many constraints from their settings, which hinder them from carrying out their anticipated practice. In Nadya's case, the constraints were caused by lack of support from her school management.

Improving teaching and learning

Mentoring assists novice teachers in improving their classroom teaching and learning activities (Hobson, Ashby, Malderez, & Tomlinson,

2009; Malderez, 2009; Strong, 2009). The findings of Evertson and Smithey's (2000) study on mentor-protégé relationships indicated that mentoring assisted protégés to develop more efficient classroom routine, deliver clearer classroom instruction, enhance pupils' participation in teaching and learning activities, and reduce pupils' misbehaviour. In the field of second language teacher education, Kissau and King (2014) discovered that beginning teachers without mentors faced difficulty in planning their lesson as compared to teacher with mentors. Likewise, the findings of the present study suggested that mentoring facilitates the novice ESL teachers to improve their classroom practices in order to accommodate the need of their particular context. As a whole, the findings showed that the novice teachers participating in this study improved their instructional practices in terms of motivating the pupils by incorporating fun elements in their activities, employing active participation in their classroom as well as in better selection of teaching materials.

Motivating pupils

Farhan's participation in the mentoring programme influenced his instructional practices in terms of the way he motivated his pupils to learn English. During the observation of TPD workshop, the native speaker mentors were seen to emphasize on motivating the pupils through fun and enjoyable teaching and learning activities as well as interesting teaching aids. During the workshops, the participating teachers were introduced to many fun teaching ideas that were able to capture pupils' interests into learning English.

The use of enjoyable teaching activities as a tool to motivate pupils could also be seen during researcher's observation on Farhan's classroom practices. Although Farhan did not use exciting games in his lesson, the simple group activity used in his lesson was interesting enough for his pupils as they appeared to be excited and engaged throughout the lesson. Farhan also used positive reinforcement by giving 'reward' to the group who has finished the task correctly. He explains,

> When one group finished, they simultaneously said, "Mr Farhan, we have finished." Farhan replied, "Here's lollipop", while pretending giving out 'invisible lollipops' to the pupils. Then, in the group, the pupils replied, "lolli lolli pop!", and they did the lollipop dance by rolling their hands, one over the other quickly. The children looked happy doing the lollipop dance as they giggled and gave each other 'high fives'.

Despite the simple lesson, the pupils seemed to be engaged and enjoy the group activity. In addition to the use of interesting teaching and learning activities to motivate his pupils, Farhan's mentor, Sally raised his awareness about the importance for him to be approachable and entertaining to young pupils so that they felt motivated to learn English. Hence, Farhan tried to entertain his pupils by cracking jokes and using funny accent. For example, during the first observation on Farhan's classroom teaching and learning activities conducted by the researcher, he was observed to use funny accent saying 'No! No! No!', when he disapproved the answer given by the pupils. Instead of being intimidated by his disapproval, the pupils laughed at his funny accent. Farhan's friendly and entertaining approach created a lively learning atmosphere, which was able to draw pupils' interest into the lesson. Farhan believed that it is crucial for teachers to include fun elements in their approach, as this would make the young pupils feel safe and comfortable during the lesson, thus motivating them to learn.

English as the medium of classroom instruction

Research in second language education has indicated that mentors played an important role in influencing novice teachers' instructional practices. In Farhan's case, his mentor Sally made him realize that it was possible to use only English for giving instructions with his Year 1 pupils. During the interview, Farhan stated that before his participation in the programme, he used Malay as the medium of classroom instruction because whenever he used English to give classroom instructions, the pupils will put on the "I-want-Malay-instructions expression". However, during team-teaching with his mentor, he noticed that the pupils were able to understand Sally's English instruction.

> When we do team-teaching, I noticed that the children can understand what the mentor want them to do. Sally has the ability to make the children understand, or participate well in the lesson without having to speak any word of Malay. So I wonder why we have to use both English and Malay when teaching. But she (Sally) did say that, sometimes, with Malay teachers the children know that they can push you until you give them instruction in Malay. But when dealing with a foreigner, the children automatically know that this teacher cannot give instruction in Malay, so they will adapt, put extra effort to understand what the foreigner say.

Realizing that his pupils could actually comprehend simple classroom instruction in English, Farhan decided to minimize the use of first language in his English lessons. Consequently, not only his Year 1 pupils were able to understand Farhan's instruction, they were also capable of constructing simple questions to him. By using simple sentences, gestures, and different intonation, Farhan carried out his teaching and learning activities in English and pupils were able to carry out his instruction. Farhan tried to limit the use of first language in his classroom; therefore, whenever the pupils used the first language during the teaching and learning activities, he rephrased his pupils' sentence in English.

More than just writing

Nadya believed that her participation in the mentoring programme influenced the way she planned her English lessons. Prior to her participation in the programme, Nadya tended to place too much emphasis on writing. This is because her school superiors required teachers to show evidence of teaching and learning activities that took place in the classroom in the form of pupils' written work. However, through activities such as TPD workshops, demo teaching and co-teaching, she realized that her mentor did not solely focus on writing but gave equal attention to all the four skills: speaking, listening, reading, and writing.

> For example, for mentor, when we carry out storytelling in the classroom, we can assess pupils' understanding or reading skills through puppet where the pupils retell the story. But for the school, they want proof and they want it in written form. If we do not have writing activity as proof, the school will assume that we are not teaching during English lessons in the class.

Although there was a discrepancy between focused language skills suggested by her mentor and by her school, Nadya decided to take her mentor's advice. She felt that it was necessary for her not to focus exclusively on teaching writing but to give equal attention to the four language skills. As a result, she changed the way she planned her lessons by including a variety of activities on reading, writing, listening, and speaking.

Communicative language teaching

As for Suzanna, one aspect of instructional practices that she believed to be influenced by her mentor was the use of communicative language teaching (CLT) approach in her lessons. According to Suzanna, her mentor, John, always reminded her to create opportunity for her pupils to use English for communicative purposes during her English lessons. Suzanna asserted that John encouraged her to incorporate more pair work and group work activities in her instructional practices. John believed that those activities provided the pupils the avenue to work together on negotiating meaning as well as promote cooperative environment among pupils. In addition, John advised Suzanna to include more speaking activities in order to give the pupils the opportunity to practise their speaking skills. Suzanna explained,

> John encourages us to prepare lessons that make pupils use the language – such as speaking activity. He would advise, yes, the lesson is good but please think about how the pupils are going to use the language. So, I have to include more speaking activities so they can speak with their friends.

At the beginning of her teaching experience as an ESL teacher, Suzanna preferred to adopt a teacher-centred approach. Suzanna felt teacher-centred approach gave her more authority in controlling her classroom as the activities gave pupils limited room to misbehave and create noise during her lessons. However, when John advised Suzanna to implement CLT approach in her lessons, she started to be aware of the value of the CLT approach in developing her pupils' oral communication skills. Through discussing with her mentor and observing his demo lessons where the communicative approach was adopted, her concern about the feasibility of CLT was allayed, and she felt more confident to put it into practice. As such, she gradually changed her instructional practices by including more CLT activities.

Teaching materials

In Nadya's case, being involved in the mentoring programme has influenced the way she selected teaching materials for her lessons. Through the various TPD workshops, Nadya learned to identify more appropriate teaching materials and to be more creative in selecting materials for her mixed-ability pupils. Prior to her participation in the programme, Nadya tended to rely solely on the prescribed textbook as her teaching materials. However, her mentors encouraged her to employ a variety of teaching materials in her English lessons. The programme also provided her the platform for exchange of ideas with other participating teachers in the TPD workshops. Nadya was able to use teaching materials shared by her colleagues through Dropbox.

Hence, this reduced her workload in preparing teaching materials, which could be tedious and time-consuming.

Nevertheless, Nadya expressed her frustration over the lack of support that she received from her school regarding teaching materials for her classroom. She complained about the difficulty in preparing teaching materials as she was unable to get her resources photocopied at school due to lack of funding. As a result, she had to photocopy her teaching resources at commercial photocopy places. In addition, Nadya faced challenges in using technology-based teaching materials due to lengthy procedures that she needed to go through in order to use computer facilities.

Despite the lack of support that Nadya received from her school, she maintained her effort in selecting, adapting, developing, and using suitable teaching resources for her lessons. For Nadya, it was important to ensure that the resources that she used for her pupils to be both interesting and valuable in promoting English language learning.

Concrete experience

Just like Nadya, Suzanna has improved the way she selected, adapted, and developed teaching materials for her English lessons. Her mentor, John, stressed on the importance of using teaching materials that could provide concrete learning experience for her pupils. In addition, he insisted that Suzanna should select teaching materials which enabled her pupils to be involved actively in the learning process. This is to ensure that the low-proficiency pupils were able to scaffold their learning by relating concrete learning experience to knowledge presented in English lesson. In order to illustrate the idea of using teaching materials to promote concrete learning experience to Suzanna and other participating teachers, John demonstrated an example of activity that he carried out with his children. In the activity, John took his toddlers to a supermarket to teach them about fruit. He brought his children to the fruits section and introduced various fruits to them. In addition, he asked them to tell him the fruits that they like and dislike. John documented this activity by recording a video, and he showed the video to Suzanna and other participating teachers during a TPD workshop as an example of an activity that provide concrete learning experience for pupils. Hence, Suzanna was determined to incorporate the use of teaching aids such as realia that promotes concrete learning experience for her pupils.

Suzanna's attempt in incorporating teaching materials that allow concrete learning experience for her pupils was seen during the second observation on her English lesson. In the lesson, Suzanna was seen taking all of her Year 2 pupils to the school recycle hut to carry out a lesson on the topic of recycling. At the recycle hut, she showed the pupils different colours of recycling bins for different types of recycling materials. While pointing at the bins, she told her pupils that blue bin is for papers, brown bin is for glass, and orange bin is for aluminium tins, steel tins and plastic. Then, she introduced her pupils with different examples of recycling items. Then, she helped the pupils to categorize the items according to their materials and the recycling bins that they belong, before returning to class to continue the lesson with speaking and writing activities on the topic of recycling. This lesson indicated Suzanna's effort in using teaching materials that promote concrete learning experience for her pupils, as suggested by her mentor.

From these case studies, we could see that the respective mentors had an impact on the novice teachers' instructional practices as they improved their teaching and learning activities.

Promoting reflective practice

Mentors are widely acknowledged as practitioners who help their mentees to learn to be reflective. They help to unpack issues of pedagogy with novice teachers so that they can critically evaluate their teaching and learning activities. Studies have shown that mentoring has a noteworthy role in the establishment of reflective practice among the teachers (Bates, Drits, & Ramirez, 2011; Feiman-Nemser, 2001; Hobson et al., 2009). Reflective practice serves as a powerful tool that promotes teachers' lifelong professional development as it allows them to evaluate their teaching in order for them to improve their professional practice (Burton, 2009).

In the present study, three out of the four novice teachers believed that their participation in the programme enabled them to engage in two kinds of reflective practice. First, supported reflective practice, where the mentors initiated novice teachers' reflective activities by assisting them to reflect on their practice through constructive feedbacks as well as templates of reflection, questionnaire, and reflective journal. Second, independent reflective practice, where the novice teachers initiated their own efforts to reflect on their practice autonomously by immersing into critical thinking and analysing about their practice.

Supported reflective practice

For Suzanna, the programme enabled her to identify her capacity as an ESL teacher through constructive feedback given by her mentors on her teaching performance. Suzanna stated that her mentors carried out observations on ten of her classroom lessons. At the end of each observed lesson, Suzanna and her mentors would have a thorough discussion on her teaching performance for that particular lesson. During the discussion, her mentors assisted her to reflect on her strengths and weaknesses in carrying out the lesson. In addition, her mentors gave her suggestions on improving her teaching and learning activities. According to Suzanna, she felt motivated by the constructive feedback given by her mentors, as they never demoralized her by giving hurtful comments on her lesson. Furthermore, she felt that her mentors respected her authority as a teacher, as they gave her freedom in making decision pertaining to her lesson.

Suzanna considered the constructive feedback given by her mentors as valuable because they encouraged her to continue reflecting on her competence as an ESL teacher. Additionally, feedback given by her mentor assisted in identifying her potentials and limitations as a teacher that she was not aware of. Hence, this allowed her to exploit her strengths in maximizing her teaching performance and to improve her weaknesses in order to develop her competence as an ESL teacher. Moreover, Suzanna was determined to minimize her weak points by trying not to repeat similar mistakes that were made during the observed lesson. When asked how her mentor has helped her to reflect on her ability, Suzanna explained,

> He gave me space to discover my own strengths and weaknesses. So through the reflection and the discussion, I would say, that's how the mentor help me to reflect on my ability. Because, sometimes we are not aware of our own strengths and weaknesses.

In addition, her mentor provided her with evaluation forms with a list of criteria, which served as a guideline for her to reflect on the effectiveness of her lessons. These allowed her to recognize her potential and limitation, thus enabling her to make necessary adjustment to improve her practice. Pitton (2006) highlights the value of constructive feedback and discussion before and after classroom observation as essential reflection to ensure successful mentoring. Likewise, Kissau and King (2014) asserted that mentors should encourage mentee-generated discussion where mentees shared their thoughts about their experiences, process in making teaching decision, and uncertainties about their practice so that mentors can respond constructively to improve mentees' practice.

Independent reflective practice

Teachers' reflective practice empowers lifelong professional development, allowing them to be critical about their teaching and improve their
teaching decisions (Burton, 2009). As for Farhan, the *Native Speaker
Programme* provided the room for him to immerse into his own thoughts
about his role as an ESL teacher. His participation in the programme
allowed him to be analytical about his teaching as he constantly made
comparison between the input given by his mentor and his own practices.
The juxtaposition enabled Farhan to make better-informed teaching decisions and adjust his practices to improve the quality of his teaching.

In addition, the TPD workshops allowed him to make a comparison of his competences as an ESL teacher with other English
teachers who participated in the programme. In the TPD workshops
that Farhan attended, participants were encouraged to collaborate
through activities such as group work and group discussion. Through
these activities, the participants were involved in constructive social
exchange where they conversed about their teaching experience in
their respective schools. In all the TPD observations carried out by
the researcher, the participating teachers appeared to enjoy sharing
anecdotes about their teaching practices with each other. Farhan utilized the social exchange that he had with other participants as a
vehicle for him to evaluate his teaching practices. This is important
for him, as he was able to compare his practices with other participating teachers.

Putnam and Borko (2000) argue that the kind of sharing that takes
place in a learning community can assist teachers "to engage in rich
discourse about important ideas" (p. 11). The programme inspired
him to continually reflect on his performance by juxtaposing his classroom practices with the input gained from the programme. Ultimately,
Farhan would make necessary adjustment to ensure that his practices
were in line with the standard established by his mentors. This finding is
aligned with Hine's (2000) assertion that mentoring promotes reflective
practice among mentees as it supported them to reflect independently,
become metacognitively attentive, and develop into self-directed learners, by participating in social interaction in their context.

In Nadya's case, her participation in the *Native Speaker Programme*
provided her the opportunity to engage in supported reflective practice and to engage in self-evaluation. She continuously questioned herself "Will they (the pupils) be entertained? Will they have fun? Will
they learn?" Additionally, she constantly assessed the suitability of
her teaching methods and materials, and made necessary adjustment
when the need arises. She said,

Because of what I have learnt during the TPD workshop, I keep asking myself to do better or to find things that is more effective to use in the classroom – that you can use to cater to your pupils. I've done this and it is not working, so I should find something else. I keep on thinking how I can modify my lesson so that I can cater to everyone or every kind of pupils, every level of proficiency.

Trivializing reflective practice

In contrast to the positive responses on reflective practices from the three novice teachers, Hafiz claimed that his mentor downplayed the value of reflective practice by carrying out reflective activities merely for the sake of documentation. Mentoring programmes such as the *Native Speaker Programme* could be a potentially powerful platform in promoting participating teachers to engage in reflective practice. Unfortunately, in Hafiz's case, this valuable opportunity was taken for granted since the participating teachers were asked to write reflection merely for the documentation purposes.

Although supported reflective practices were conducted where mentees were required to fill out reflective journal and questionnaire on their progress, Hafiz's mentor did not provide any response to mentees' reflections. Every month, his mentor will collect the reflective journals from his mentees, so that he could examine them and take necessary action requested by the teachers. In the journal, Hafiz recorded the strengths and weaknesses of his lessons and he included teaching aspects that he felt essential for his mentor to provide him with extra guidance. Most of the time, he requested for more input on classroom management and teaching ideas for extremely weak pupils. In the beginning, Hafiz was very motivated to write critical reflective entries on his teaching activities, expecting that Nate would read the entries and gave him additional assistance on classroom management and teaching ideas for extremely weak pupils. However, after a few entries, he began to lose the enthusiasm to write critical reflection as he realized that Nate did not provide him with adequate support that he needed when he felt helpless dealing with problems related to classroom management and extremely weak pupils.

When we write the reflective journal, they ask us what we want to improve on, and sometimes I just write down, but I don't think they read my reflection. Because I always ask them how to control class…issues with weak pupils… But they never do activities that cater to my need…that I require. Maybe the reflective journal is just for them to see. For documentation….

Not only that, Hafiz's mentor insisted his mentees to give higher ratings in the evaluation forms to indicate that they have progressed throughout the programme despite their actual performance. Hence, this gave Hafiz and other teachers the impression that reflective practice was unimportant and thus underrating its true value. Numerous studies have shown that mentors have the tendency to place too much emphasis on their role in transmitting knowledge on teaching and learning to their mentees, thus neglecting their potential in promoting reflective practice, which is important for their lifelong professional development (Hobson et al., 2009). Rippon and Martin (2006) argue that whether a mentor is able to facilitate reflective practices and collaboration depends on the quality of their interaction, which, in turn, relies on the mentor's personality and knowledge.

In conclusion, the findings of the study for this category revealed two main conclusions. First, mentors played a vital role in influencing novice teachers' classroom practices. This is drawn based on the findings that mentors in this programme positively influenced novice teachers' classroom management, ways of motivating students, teaching methodology, and selection of teaching materials. Second, the mentoring programme serves as medium for novice teachers to engage in reflective practice. This conclusion is drawn based on the finding that three out of the four participants asserted that their participation in the *Native Speaker Programme* facilitated them to engage in critical reflection.

8   Professional identity
    formation through mentoring

In this chapter, we shall report findings from a study on the impact of mentoring on novice ESL teachers' professional identity formation. Miller (2009) asserts that in the field of TESOL, identity has been used as a concept to explore questions about the sociocultural contexts of learning and learners, pedagogy, language ideologies, and the ways in which language and discourses work to marginalize or empower speakers.

Based on Pennington and Richards' (2016) notion of teacher identity, four dimensions of professional identity formation were identified from our data. These dimensions include *professional identity* which is defined by teachers' disciplinary knowledge and accountability, *personal identity* which refers to teacher's capacity in identifying their strengths and weaknesses, *membership in communities of practices identity* which is influenced by contextual factors, *student-related identity* which is greatly influenced by teachers' knowledge and awareness about pupils, and lastly, *language-related identity* which relates to teachers' language background and language proficiency.

Professional identity

In this study, the *Native Speaker Programme* serves as a platform for the novice ESL teachers to construct their professional identity. Leung (2009) posits that there are two different dimensions to professionalism. The first is the institutionally prescribed and what quality instructional practices should consist of. These involve procedures for achieving accountability and maintain quality teaching. The second dimension is the *independent professionalism*. This refers to teachers' views and conscious reflection of their teaching practices.

Accountability

One of the impacts, which the mentoring programme seemed to have on the novice ESL teachers' professional identity formation, was in developing their accountability towards the teaching profession. Nadya, Farhan, and Suzanna believed that their participation in the *Native Speaker Programme* influenced them to be more responsible, passionate, and conscientious towards their duties as ESL teachers.

For Nadya, her participation in the mentoring programme enabled her to experience changes in her identity as an ESL teacher. The programme developed her passion towards teaching as her mentor continually encouraged her to be enthusiastic about teaching English to young learners. From someone who was being 'forced' to take up teaching as a profession, Nadya transformed into a passionate ESL teacher during the programme. When asked on how her mentor assisted her in understanding her identity as an ESL teacher, Nadya had the following to say:

> Basically, she teaches you not to be a teacher but to be an educator. Being an educator means to make sure that your pupils understand what you have taught, they use the language, and you care about things inside and outside the classroom. That's what she has taught us. And being educator means you have passion, you need to be passionate about pupils learning.

As for Farhan, the mentoring programme assisted him to develop a sense of responsibility in his duty as an ESL teacher, an important quality that was absent in his first year of teaching experience. Farhan claimed that the hardship, which he experienced, negatively influenced his performance as a teacher. His recollection on his attitudes during the first teaching post in a very rural school, made him realize that he was "not a good teacher. I created excuses...I have to go through all these so, when I go to class, I just do whatever I can, whatever I want. Not really what I am capable of". However, when he moved to a new school and was required to participate in the *Native Speaker Programme*, Farhan became motivated to be more responsible towards his duty as ESL teacher, through inspiring examples set by his mentors. He remarks:

> The (mentors) skills, their work ethics are something that I really look up to. I think they (mentors) are really hardworking, really focused in doing things for the children. They are very determined.

Those are good qualities, work ethics that they have shown us. I think I should take it as an example that I should try to do.

Farhan acknowledged that the programme and his native speaker mentors have helped him to be a conscientious teacher. He also believed that his positive attitude towards the programme enabled him to benefit from it, particularly in constructing his professional identity as a responsible teacher. Like Farhan, Hafiz's participation in the *Native Speaker Programme* influenced his professional identity as a teacher, as he wished to adopt certain positive work ethics shown by his mentor. Hafiz felt that his time management was appalling. He never really cared about his poor time management since most people he knew had the same attitude with him pertaining to time management. However, Hafiz's participation in the programme provided him an eye-opening experience about the value of time. His mentors' good time management skills made him realize that punctuality and good time management have a positive impact on productivity. Hence, Hafiz wished to adopt this positive work ethics as part of his professional identity because he believed that it would improve his productivity as an ESL teacher. He elaborates:

> In terms of work ethic, time management. Nate is very punctual. When he says it's 9, it is going to be exactly at 9. Even the TPD session, if they said 2.30, they will look at their watch, right at 2.30 they will start. And they will finish sharp at 5.30. Unlike us, Malaysians, we have plus minus, if we say 5.30, sometimes we finish early. If they finish earlier for 5 minutes, they will come up with other activity. Very punctual. So, that is something good that we can adopt into our work ethics.

Similarly, Suzanna believed it was through this mentoring programme, she managed to develop her sense of accountability towards her job. Through the guidance that she received from her mentors as well as through her interaction with other participating teachers in the programme, she became more conscientious of her role as a teacher. Suzanna started her first year of teaching with a certainty that she was going to be able to carry out her responsibilities as an ESL teacher effectively. However, she found herself questioning about her own competency when she experienced a few challenges in the rural primary school where she worked. According to Suzanna, the most challenging problem that she experienced when she first started teaching in her school was related to classroom management and the new KSSR curriculum. While classroom management problem is common and expected among novice teachers, Suzanna also faced difficulty with the content of the subject that she needed to teach. She was not familiar with the newly introduced KSSR curriculum. Suzanna explained:

> Classroom management, because I was teaching Year 1, last class, with new KSSR curriculum. So I faced two challenges. I have to deal with the new KSSR curriculum and classroom management.

Suzanna believed that the struggles that she experienced at the beginning of her teaching career adversely affected her teaching performance. With the combination of the implementation of the new curriculum, classroom management problems, extremely low-proficiency learners, and the extra hours that she needed to spend as a participant in the *Native Speaker Programme*, Suzanna felt that she needed to adapt to so many things. Because of the difficulties that she needed to face, Suzanna felt that it was challenging to give her best and maximize her potential. This, in turn, disappointed her and decreased her motivation to carry out her responsibility as an ESL teacher effectively.

Throughout the study, Suzanna's conscientiousness on her duty as an ESL teacher was seen through her determination in ensuring her pupils' good achievement. As an English teacher who was teaching lower primary pupils (Year 1 to Year 3), she heard many negative comments from the upper primary (Year 4 to Year 6) English teachers. They questioned the accountability of lower primary English teachers in teaching the lower primary pupils about basic English skills. This is because they found that most of the lower primary pupils entered the upper primary years with very limited English skills. This situation posed problems for them to proceed with higher-level language content, as the pupils did not master even the basic skills. Realizing these shortcomings in basic English skills among the lower primary pupils, Suzanna determined to carry out her duty diligently. She wanted her pupils to have a good mastery of basic English skills so that they could proceed with learning higher-level language skills at the upper primary levels without difficulties.

Student-related identity

Pennington and Richards (2016) assert that knowledge and awareness of the learners are regarded as central elements of teaching competence in teachers' professional identity construction. Knowledge and awareness about students assist the teachers in making any pedagogical decision on the best way to teach their foreign language learners within complex socially, culturally, and historically situated contexts (Borg, 2003; Johnson, 2006; Woods, 1996).

From the case studies, all of the participants seemed to believe that their native speaker mentors had an impact on them in terms of guiding them to be more approachable, understanding, and empathetic towards their pupils. They also learnt to be more tolerant with pupils' limitations and establish good rapport with the pupils.

Farhan experienced changes in his student-related identity formation, as he felt more compassionate towards his young ESL learners. Recollecting the experience when he was first assigned to teach English to seven-year-old primary school pupils, he admitted that he was too harsh with them. He believes his lack of understanding about young learners as one of the factors that led to his rigid and strict approach, which included using a cane to punish the pupils. Prior to his participation in the mentoring programme, he found that it was difficult to deal with small children, as they were "rowdy" and "naughty". Furthermore, the fact that he had to face major changes where he was required to implement the new KSSR curriculum and at the same time assigned to be a class teacher for the Year 1 pupils also led to anxiety which contributed to his punitive approach towards his Year 1 pupils.

However, Farhan's rigid approach towards his young pupils had changed since his participation in the programme as his mentor, Sally, continuously inspired him to be more compassionate towards his pupils. As a result, he was able to be "more understanding and less strict" as well as to adapt his teaching styles to suit the young learners with the help from his mentor. He said:

> After joining the Native Speaker Programme, my mentor, Sally, guided me how to carry out lessons, she shed some lights on activities for young kids and how I should approach little children. So, when I got some help and I see what the children need actually, gradually I changed my approach. My mentor helped me to change the way I teach, the way I deal with the kids.

Farhan now viewed himself as more approachable and more 'suitable' as an English teacher for the Year 1 pupils. Likewise, he believed that his pupils felt comfortable and safe with him and he is trying to be funny and interesting around them. He also aspires to create a comfortable environment for his pupils to learn English effectively.

Similarly, Suzanna believed that the *Native Speaker Programme* enabled her to experience changes in her identity as an ESL teacher, as she became more compassionate towards her pupils. Through the advice given by her mentor, Suzanna became more tolerant towards her pupils with extremely low level of language proficiency. Suzanna stated that in her first year of teaching, she did not take into account her pupils' differences in language proficiency when conducting teaching and learning activities. She explained:

> My mentors always keep on reminding me not to neglect the weak pupils. When I am teaching the weaker class, they noticed that I have the tendency to leave the weaker pupils behind. Because sometimes it was difficult to include them in all the activities. So my mentors reminded me to make sure I monitor the weak ones. Make sure they get what I teach, to be more compassionate with those lower proficiency pupils. Don't ignore them because that is unfair.

After her mentors informed her about her unhealthy practice, Suzanna became aware that she needed to be more tolerant toward the less capable pupils and pay more attention to their needs.

In Hafiz's case, he believed that his mentor has taught him to become more empathetic towards his low-proficiency pupils. According to Hafiz, prior to his participation in the programme, he placed too much emphasis on finishing the syllabus. As he rushed through the syllabus, trying to cover all the topics and contents in the English language curriculum specifications, he overlooked his pupils' preferences, language proficiency, and needs. Fortunately, Hafiz started to take into consideration his pupils' ability and interest as Nate convinced him to focus more on pupils' learning rather than on finishing the syllabus. The following excerpt denotes how Hafiz's mentor changed Hafiz's priority in teaching:

> Last year, before this programme, I rushed through my lessons because I wanted to finish the entire syllabus. But now, Nate told me it's okay, if we don't finish it. Once the pupils get it, I would then proceed with the next thing.

In addition, Hafiz's participation in the programme enabled him to develop more empathy towards his low-proficiency pupils as he changed his belief about pupils' accomplishment in language learning. Before participating in the programme, Hafiz employed an exam-oriented approach, as he was very concerned about his pupils' performance in examinations and tests. As a result, his lessons were uninteresting and stressful as he 'forced' his low-proficiency pupils to learn. However, through his mentors' guidance on the use of fun and interesting teaching and learning activities, Hafiz realized that examinations are not the only tools to measure his pupils' accomplishment in learning English. Hence, Hafiz adopted a more relaxed approach and this reflected in his empathy towards his low-proficiency pupils.

Furthermore, his mentor helped him to become more sensitive towards his pupils as he gained a better insight about young learners. Through his mentor, Hafiz realized that he needed to take into consideration about his pupils' limited literacy skills when planning lessons and selecting teaching materials. For example, before his participation in the programme, Hafiz preferred to use word cards as teaching aids for his Year 2 pupils. However, his mentor suggested that he use the whiteboard and manually write the word so that his pupils could see the steps of writing clearly. This would assist the low-proficiency pupils who did not have basic skills in writing alphabets to identify the steps needed in order to form each word correctly.

Moreover, Hafiz also developed a more empathetic position towards his low-proficiency pupils as he changed his teaching role from a strict 'authoritarian' to a more approachable 'facilitator'. Hafiz used to opt for rote learning activities where he played the traditional roles as a teacher. Nonetheless, through the guidance that he received from his mentor, Hafiz switched to a more pupil-centred teaching activity where he played the role as a facilitator who assisted pupils' learning. As Hafiz changed his teaching approach, his lessons became more relaxed and he would take into account his pupils' preference and interest in selecting his teaching and learning activities.

Personal identity

Mentoring enhances novice teachers' self-confidence

Another important impact of mentoring on the novice ESL teachers' professional identity formation is by enhancing their self-confidence. Numerous research (Hobson, Ashby, Malderez, & Tomlinson, 2009; Ingersoll & Strong, 2011; Izadinia, 2015; Ticknor, 2014) acknowledged the roles of mentoring in imparting positive self-perception to the mentees. All of the participants agreed that their participation in the Native Speaker Mentoring Programme helped them to enhance their self-confidence.

For Nadia, having involved in the programme helped her to develop her confidence in her own capability to teach English effectively. Reflecting to her first year of teaching prior to the programme, Nadya disclosed that she was uncertain about her ability to teach effectively. She always had doubts and questioned herself, "Am I doing this right? Will I be able to teach the kids? Are they getting the right information from me?" Nadya realized that she had limited procedural skills to teach English to young learners effectively. Through the *Native Speaker Programme*, her mentor helped her in making the most of her existing knowledge thus improving herself as an ESL teacher. She said,

> I have the basic knowledge, being guided by my mentor, make me even better. Because, I have the good foundation, and then, this mentor helps me to exploit my base – to be a better teacher.

In addition, Nadya's confidence as an ESL teacher increased, as she is now able to rationalize the teaching and learning activities selected for her pupils. This is because in the TPD workshops, Nadya was taught to select teaching and learning activities based on her learners' needs and preferences. Nadya admitted that having school superiors who were always sceptical about her lessons used to lower her self-esteem. However, she is now able to provide good justification for her choices of teaching and learning activities to her school superiors. She was assured of her decisions concerning teaching and she was confident about her competence as an ESL teacher.

Suzanna maintains that her participation in the *Native Speaker Programme* enhanced her self-confidence as she felt that her mentors respect her authority as an ESL teacher. According to Suzanna, John and Stella's positive mentoring styles that put trust in her capability as an ESL teacher, contributed to her self-confidence. Initially, Suzanna was worried if the programme would mirror her daunting practicum experience, where her lessons were severely criticized by her lecturers. The experience robbed her self-confidence, as she continually doubted whether she has what it takes to be an effective teacher. However, her worry was proven pointless as she participated in the programme since she never received demoralizing comments on her capacity as an ESL teacher. Instead, she found the feedback given by her mentors on her lessons to be helpful for her professional development. According to Suzanna, her mentors always gave her freedom in making decision related to teaching. Her mentors' approval of her teaching capabilities enhanced her self-confidence. Suzanna's experience illustrated that the recognition she received from her native speaker mentors affirmed her identity as an ESL teacher and she felt empowered through having her mentors' validation. As a result, the mentoring programme assisted her to increase her self-confidence as part of her professional identity as an ESL teacher.

Research (Feiman-Nemser, 2001; Harrison, Dymoke, & Pell, 2006; Patrick, 2013) shows that it is important for mentors to provide mentees with suitable degree of independence in order to facilitate them to form their teaching style that defines who they are as teachers.

Membership in communities of practices

Mentoring promotes positive perception about the teaching profession

According to Bieler (2013), having a strong sense of identity allows novice teachers to be autonomous and stay strong during their first years of teaching which results in teacher retention. Studies (Blase, 2009; Dyson, Albon, & Hutchinson, 2007) have shown that positive experience during the first year of teaching motivated novice teachers to remain in the profession and made them feel appreciated and gain a sense of achievement. The findings from the case studies indicated the important role of mentoring in transforming the novice ESL teachers' professional identity through the promotion of positive perception about the teaching profession.

All of the novice teachers discovered that their participation in the programme provided them with positive teaching experience, which made them feel more content with their career as primary school ESL teachers. The recognition and acknowledgement, which they received from their mentors and other participating teachers, affected their feelings of belonging and membership to that community.

For Nadya, she felt more content with her job as an ESL teacher as she started to develop love for teaching during her participation in the programme. From someone who considered teaching as her 'last choice of profession' and was forced by her father to enrol into the teacher education programme, Nadya admitted that now she enjoyed being an ESL teacher. While she felt that her teacher training was ineffective in cultivating her interest towards teaching, her participation in the programme succeeded in developing her passion towards her teaching profession. Nadya considered the programme to be 'life-changing' because it made her realize that teaching is indeed a rewarding profession. Nadya's happiness and excitement demonstrated that she cared about her learners and felt fulfilled with her teaching career. She notes:

> I was really interested in teaching but the (Native Speaker) pro-gramme is really life-changing. It really changed me in terms of...I began to love this profession more, and I am not going to leave anytime soon or change career. Because I love to be with kids and I love to see them able to talk with their friends in the English language. It is like, watching your own kids growing up. Your own satisfaction, your own motivation.

Likewise, Farhan stated that he now enjoyed teaching English to his young learners. While he did not deny the difficulties and challenges that he had to face in teaching English language to his rural pupils, Farhan considered his teaching profession to be exceptionally reward-ing. Farhan acknowledged that there would be more challenges that he needs to face in the future, due to the dynamic nature of teaching profession. Nevertheless, with the knowledge and skills that he gained throughout the mentoring programme, he was positive that he would last in the teaching profession. When asked the question "Where do you see yourself in another 5 years?". Farhan answered:

> First thing, I am quite content with what I am doing, with where I am now. So in five years time, I think I will still be here. But, as a better teacher, more resourceful, more creative, more exciting, more effective. I will try to do that!

Hence, these case studies affirm existing literature that argues mentor-ing enhances retention among the novice teachers (Ingersoll & Smith, 2011; Odell & Ferraro, 1992) as it promotes positive views towards their teaching profession and enhanced their level of satisfaction with their teaching career.

Language-related identity

Embracing their 'non-nativeness'

One of the main concerns in language teacher development, which has received a lot of attention, is the role of the native speaker (Kramsch, 1997). This is due to the issues of English language teachers' compe-tencies and roles for native and non-native speakers (Medgyes, 1994; Moussu & Llurda, 2008). Pennington and Richards (2016) argue that second language teachers might 'focus on their non-native status and feel concerned about their language' (p. 12).

Farhan expressed his feeling of inadequacy concerning his speaking fluency as a non-native teacher as compared to the native speaker mentors at the beginning of his participation in the *Native Speaker Programme*. At the initial stage of his involvement in the programme, he believed that most of the mentees including himself felt 'inadequate and shy' about their level of English proficiency. They found it quite challenging to comprehend their mentors due to their thick accent. The three mentors came from different English-speaking countries: Sally from England, Ian from Ireland, and Jack from the United States. Similarly, they could sense that their mentors had difficulty in understanding their Malaysian English. Gradually, they began to familiarize themselves with each other's accent and the mentors consciously modify their native accent to make it comprehensible for their non-native mentees.

When asked if he was striving for a native-like fluency, Farhan stated that he did not wish to achieve the native-like accent even though he felt inadequate with his English language fluency. He believed that having a native-like accent would cause himself to be incomprehensible to his pupils and his colleagues. Hence, Farhan was more comfortable embracing his non-nativeness without trying too much to strive for native-like accent. He said,

> Because if you are trying to achieve native speaker's accent, you will make yourself incomprehensible to others in Malaysian context. As a teacher, you want to make yourself comprehensible to others, not only to your colleagues, but also to the children.

Farhan wished "to be able to speak at least maybe 80 per cent grammatically correct and with 80 per cent correct pronunciation. That is good enough for me I think". He believed that it is important for him to speak English regularly, as it is a crucial part of his professional identity as an ESL teacher. For Farhan, the *Native Speaker Programme* enhanced his confidence as an ESL teacher as his speaking skills improved throughout the programme. As an ESL teacher in rural school, Farhan did not have much opportunity to practise his speaking skills with his colleagues, as he did not want to be labelled as arrogant by the people around him. Although Farhan used English during his lessons with his young learners, Farhan did not think it improved his speaking skills. On the other hand, being a participant in the mentoring programme provided him the opportunity to practise his speaking skills with his native speaker mentors. Through this opportunity, Farhan was able to engage in authentic conversation with his mentors, which in turn, enabled him to improve his proficiency. Now that Farhan realized that his speaking skills have improved, he became more confident with his capacity as an ESL teacher.

As an ESL teacher in a rural school, Nadya was reluctant to use English language in her daily conversation with her local colleagues because she did not want to be labelled as someone who was trying to be a '*Mat Salleh*' (native speaker) as it would create a barrier between herself and her teaching community. Although she has a good command of English and used to speak the language in her daily exchange with her university friends, Nadya chose to minimize the use of English in her rural environment. Nadya believed by doing this, she would be able to blend in with the culture of the school and her colleagues would accept her as one of them. However, this perception changed as she participated in the *Native Speaker Programme*. During the programme, her mentor, Victoria, continually expressed the notion that English is just for communication and the language does not exclusively belong to the native English speakers. Victoria encouraged her mentees including Nadya to embrace their identity as a non-native English speaker. Gradually, Nadya began to accept the idea that English language is not necessarily associated with one's nativeness. She realized that working closely with her mentor, who is a native speaker of English language, would not change her identity as a non-native ESL teacher.

When asked if she was striving for a native-like accent, Nadya asserted that she did not wish to achieve native-like accent, as she was more comfortable with the way she is now. Nadya stated that although other people may regard her as a '*Mat Salleh*' as she was speaking more English, it would not inhibit her from using the language in daily conversation. This is because she believed that English is for everyone and speaking English does not change one's identity. She said,

> ...even though you are fluent, you are still using your own identity. You won't be a *Mat Salleh* just because the way you speak.

In Hafiz's case, he used to feel inferior as compared to the native speakers since he did not have the native-like accent. Hafiz used to believe that native speakers of English (NES) make better English language teachers. However, his belief changed as he participated in the *Native Speaker Programme*, when he noticed the limitations that the native speakers would have as English language teachers. According to Hafiz, one of the challenges would be their lack of understanding about the needs and problems of the non-native pupils. He argued that his mentor often suggested activities that were not suitable to the Malaysian learners as they contained language items that were too difficult for them. As he identified the limitations of his native speaker mentor, he also recognized the strengths of non-native ESL teachers.

Hafiz believed that non-native teachers are more sensitive to the needs and problems of the foreign language learners. Thus, they are able to plan teaching and learning activities that cater to the needs of their EFL learners. Hafiz also felt that non-native teachers could better predict language difficulties faced by their EFL pupils as compared to the native speaker mentors and identify suitable teaching approach for their learners.

Hafiz gained his newfound insight about the strengths of non-native ESL teachers through his observations of TPD workshops, which he attended. During the workshops, Hafiz found that most of the time, other participants of the programme who were mostly non-native teachers, could come up with teaching ideas that were more appropriate than the ones suggested by the mentors. Hafiz gained a lot of input from the other participating teachers, particularly in choosing suitable teaching and learning activities for his pupils. As a result, it made him realize that both native mentors and non-native teachers have their own strengths and weaknesses. While native speakers are better in terms of English language competency, Hafiz felt that the non-native ESL teachers have better contextual knowledge since they understand the needs of their non-native learners.

In conclusion, all four novice teachers who participated in the *Native Speaker Programme* felt strongly about their identity as a non-native speaker English teacher. Canagarajah (1999) points out that a large number of English teachers in the world are not native speakers of English and it is not necessary to have a native-like command of a language in order to teach it well.

9   Revisiting the novice ESL teachers' mentoring programme

In this concluding chapter, we shall revisit the notion of mentoring novice teachers and discuss the ways in which the case studies in previous chapters have enlightened our understanding of how novice ESL teachers' professional knowledge construction, practice, and identity formation developed during the Native Speaker Mentoring Programme.

First, the case studies have indicated that the *Native Speaker Programme* expanded the novice teachers' knowledge base as ESL teachers by enabling them to construct their professional knowledge with the support and expert guidance from their mentors. Most importantly, the programme contributed to novice teachers' professional knowledge by providing them the opportunity to engage in collaborative learning activities in their professional learning communities.

Secondly, the findings suggest that the *Native Speaker Programme* contributed to novice ESL teachers' professional practice by becoming reflective practitioners. The novice teachers not only engaged in supported reflective practices, but they also initiated in their own independent reflective practices. Finally, the findings of the study found that the *Native Speaker Programme* enabled the novice ESL teachers to experience changes in their professional identity formation in terms of encouraging them to embrace their identity as non-native English teachers, increasing their accountability as ESL teachers and enhanced their satisfaction about their teaching profession.

The findings from the case studies discussed in the previous chapters have highlighted some concerns with regard to the novice ESL teachers' mentoring programme in the Malaysian context. To address these changes, we propose several initiatives to support the professionalization of novice teachers in the complex social, cultural settings where they learn and work. First, we argue that there is an absence of investment in mentors' professional development, which can enhance the effectiveness of the mentoring programme. We believe that there must be concerted efforts towards improving the quality of mentors. Investment in mentors' professional development can help build teaching capacity for both mentors and mentees. Second, we believe that there is a need to create structures to support the culture of teacher learning and help them grow. Continuous high-quality professional learning can potentially provide novice teachers with the support they need to increase their competency and improve their professional practices. We argue for providing alternative practices that support the novice teachers' professional development in the "complex social, political, economic and cultural settings where they learn and work" (Johnson, 2009). Third, we believe that the mentoring programme could have an impact and shape the construction of novice ESL teachers' professional identities in various dimensions. Mentors could explicitly promote teacher identity formation through ways in which non-native teachers construct and claim ownership of their instructional practices, intercultural competence, and language skills.

In the next sections, we discuss the issues and changes that need to be made in the novice teachers' mentoring programme with specific reference to the Malaysian context.

Quality of mentors

The provision of highly prepared and effective mentors contributes to the success of novice teachers during the period of professional development. Mentoring will not positively affect the novice teachers if the mentors are not well prepared for their role (He, 2009). It is important for teacher development programmes to screen and train mentors in terms of their professional competence, interpersonal and intercultural skills in order to maximize the benefits of mentoring programmes.

Data from the case studies in Chapter 6 indicated that the mentoring programme furnished the novice teachers' professional knowledge construction through the effective roles of their mentors, which include facilitator, speaking partner, source of reference, the native model, and agent of change. For instance, Farhan believed that his mentor's thoughtfulness enabled him to maximize his learning throughout the programme. According to Farhan, he was comfortable with Sally's mentoring style because it brought positive vibes during activities and making it stress-free for him. The good rapport that was established between Sally and Farhan allowed them to communicate well with each other, hence making the mentoring activities more effective. This finding corroborates with previous studies (Delaney, 2012; Izadinia, 2015) that have identified effective mentor personal qualities as responsible, supportive, and having non-confrontational style.

Previous research (Feiman-Nemser, 2001; Maynard, 2000; Rippon & Martin, 2006) has shown that the establishments of emotional and psychological support are essential in ensuring effective mentoring so that the mentees feel welcome, accepted, and included. In this study, the emotional and psychological supports were provided by the mentors particularly for Nadya and Suzanna. Nadya regarded her mentor, Victoria, as dedicated as she exhibited great enthusiasm in helping Nadya to confront challenges that she faced as a novice teacher. In addition, Nadya considered Victoria as a very considerate mentor as she allowed her mentees to bring along their children to the TPD workshop as well as arranged for some activities and refreshment for the children. As a result, Nadya felt motivated to participate actively in the programme.

The results from the case studies lend further support to the idea that mentors play an important role as facilitators and as agents of change to the novice teachers. Farhan considered his mentor as facilitator who 'shed some lights' as he was struggling with his duties as an ESL teacher. Likewise, Suzanna regarded her mentor as the agent of change who assisted her in going through massive transformation, as she needed to deal with new changes pertaining to implementing the new KSSR syllabus and teaching low-proficiency pupils. Both of these roles, facilitator and agent of change, are crucial in supporting the novice teachers in adapting into their new responsibilities as ESL teachers.

On the other hand, the case studies also revealed the less positive sides of some mentors' personal qualities such as being inexperienced in dealing with ESL learners and intimidating towards their mentees, could hinder the novice teachers' professional development. Having inadequate knowledge on ESL learners inhibits some of the mentors from playing effective roles in supporting novice teachers' learning, thus adversely affecting the quality of ESL mentoring. In Hafiz's case for example, his mentor did not have adequate knowledge of ESL learners in Malaysian context. As a result, Hafiz found that most of the teaching and learning activities suggested by his mentor to be inappropriate for his low-proficiency learners.

Other less positive experiences faced by the novice teachers include external issues such as lack of support from their schools, colleagues, and surroundings. These negative factors denied some of the participants full access to a conducive learning environment and delayed them from advancing throughout the five phases of Maynard and Furlong's (1995) novice teacher development stages. As a result, while some of the novice teachers had a smooth sailing progress, some had to move back and forth between phases. Hence, the current study highlights the need for mentors to be well trained for their role.

Mentoring programmes should incorporate coaching skills training. One of the concerns highlighted in this programme was that some of the native speaker mentors lacked effective mentoring skills in order to assume their roles as mentors. This issue has been raised by the Malaysian English Language Teacher Association report (2010) with regard to the qualifications of the native speaker mentors selected for the *Native Speaker Programme*. Hall (2012) rightly points out that being a native speaker does not necessarily mean a teacher is skilled as a language teacher. Neither a teacher with two or three years of teaching experience can be considered as an expert. An appointment of an expert teacher or a mentor would require relevant qualifications and experiences.

Concerns regarding limited cultural awareness and contextual knowledge were also highlighted as these native speaker mentors need to be familiar with knowledge of the Malaysian educational system and the cultural background of the learners. As some of the native speaker mentors did not have prior teaching experience in Malaysia, it was challenging for them to train the novice teachers in an unfamiliar context. Shulman (1987) rightly points out that knowledge of learners and educational contexts are important in understanding teachers' knowledge base.

Therefore, there is a need for teacher educators to provide an avenue to empower mentors in developing their mentoring skills as well as their awareness about their accountability as mentors. As Vikaraman, Mansor, and Hamzah (2017) argue, "effective mentoring and adequate administrative support are important factors to sustain quality of teaching for beginner teachers and taking up responsibilities as teacher leaders" (p. 167).

Strategies to support the culture of teacher learning

A focus on the nature of teacher learning is central to a mentoring programme. Teacher learning from traditional perspective is seen as a cognitive issue, where the focus is on improving the teaching effectiveness. From the situated learning perspective, learning takes place in a context and evolves through the interaction and participation of the participants in the context. Teacher learning is viewed as constructing new knowledge and theory through participants in specific social contexts and engaging in particular types of activities and processes. Learning is seen to emerge through social interaction within a community of practice. This marks a shift in novice teachers' development away from traditional transmissive teacher development towards participation, construction, and becoming a member of teaching community.

Professional communities of practice

Mentoring programmes can provide opportunities for novice teachers to look closely at teaching through specific activities in their communities of practice. First, professional development programmes can help novice teachers to develop collegial relationships with their peers. The surrounding community of teachers may be the best source of learning and support for new teachers. Greater collegiality in the profession has been identified as a key goal for supporting novice teachers. Novice teachers can tap into the collective experience of the profession through close, sustained contact with a more experienced mentor or peers. Peer observations, peer reflection, and joint inquiry workshops all reinforce the idea that novices can learn from one another. Novice teachers in their early years tend to rely upon their connections with other teachers. Thus, it is fitting that approaches to support that go beyond mentoring look to facilitate and improve these connections. Good professional development should engage teachers in collaboration problem-solving; should be continuous, supported, information rich; and should help teachers develop a theoretical understanding of the elements involved in the change or reform (Hawley & Valli, 1999).

Richter et al.'s (2013) study has shown that mentoring strategies that employ transformative approach are successful in producing novice teachers who are effective, enthusiastic, satisfied, and contented, as compared to mentoring strategies that employed transmissive approach. The present study provides support to this finding as the participants identified transformative mentoring strategies promote professional communities of practice, exchange of ideas among participants, learning by doing, hands-on input, and peer teaching as effective in assisting their professional knowledge construction as compared to transmissive strategies such as lecture-based sessions on theoretical input and grammatical rules during TPD workshops.

The findings of the present study indicated that one of the effective ESL mentoring strategies is to promote the exchange of ideas among participating teachers in the *Native Speaker Programme*. Two participants in the study, Nadya and Hafiz, asserted that the programme contributed to their professional knowledge construction through collaboration, interaction, and reflection with other participating teachers in the programme. Hobson, Ashby, Malderez, and Tomlinson (2009) maintain that novice teachers' mentoring would be more effective if it promotes collegial learning culture where the teachers in similar or different schools are given the opportunity to interact with each other.

The present study also identified peer teaching as another effective mentoring strategy that contributed to novice teachers' professional knowledge construction. Suzanna asserted that through peer teaching, she was able to gain better understanding on the correct ways to conduct certain teaching and learning activities as she and her peers would together plan, carry out, and reflect on the lessons. In the Malaysian context, one of the strategies that have been initiated by the MOE to improve the teaching profession is to implement the Professional Learning Community approach in schools across the country in 2011. The main idea of PLCs is to engage with the notion of developing the potential of every person that contributes to school improvement. Thus, collaboration among teachers as peers in a school environment is essential to create the opportunity of sharing, coaching, and cooperating towards school improvement (Morel, 2014).

Online platform

Mentoring programme has been viewed as an essential tool that supports the learning and growth of novice teachers. Good mentoring programmes should create conditions for developing vital skills that can be learned only from practice. We should create opportunities for novice teachers to gain knowledge and understandings that they could not learn in their teacher education programme (Feiman-Nemser, 2003). The purpose should be developing effective teachers, a strong teaching force, a vital profession, and optimum learning for students in schools. Mentoring programme should be developed with the assumption that novice teachers need different approaches and formats to support the broad range of learning and development required of them.

Recent changes brought about by developments in technology have introduced the use of online platform for professional development programmes to provide an additional support to the novice teachers. E-mentoring allows greater flexibility than traditional, face-to-face mentoring since it is time and place independent. Applied to novice teacher professional development, e-mentoring provides greater opportunities for participants to connect and interact with colleagues in and across a variety of settings. Blended programmes could also be one solution to meet the demand for mentoring programme in a diverse range of contexts and situations. One of the initiatives could be in the form of both face-to-face communities of teachers (Hanson-Smith, 2006) and online communities (Kabilan, Adlina, & Embi, 2011). Online networking could facilitate sharing among members of the teaching community. Barabási (2002) claims that it makes connections between people more efficient and widespread sharing of information. Through networking, teachers can disseminate ideas through larger numbers and keep those ideas from only being shared through one central hub. Moreover, this strategy could also alleviate potential isolation among new teachers.

Critical reflective practices

Farrell (2015) suggests that novice teachers' development of teaching skills could be promoted through reflective practice. He argues that reflective practice is based on the assumption that teachers learn from experience through "systematic and focused reflection on the nature and meaning of teaching experiences" (2015, p. 194). As such, the mentors should encourage novice teachers to think deeply about specific aspects of teaching or engage with issues that they face in their own classrooms, i.e. the challenges of planning, the design of learning tasks, the management of new curriculum, and the dilemmas of assessment.

Mentors can facilitate novice teachers to look closely at their own practice by focusing on reflection and inquiry activities. They can also push novice teachers to examine their own classroom practices by creating activities that focus on reflection and inquiry. The practice of reflection allows novice teachers to be aware of their own practices, avoid possible mistakes, and thus develop a set of strategies to implement positive classroom changes or practices. Kabilan (2007) rightly points out that sharing of critical reflective practices serves as a vital link between the novice teachers' knowledge base and their ability to translate the knowledge into meaningful classroom engagement.

The findings from the case studies revealed the potential of mentoring programme in providing novice teachers the opportunity to engage in reflective practice. Reflective practice serves as a powerful tool that promotes teachers' lifelong professional development, as it allows them to evaluate their teaching autonomously in order for them to improve their practice (Burton, 2009). The study found that mentoring promotes novice teachers with two kinds of reflective practice:

supported reflective practice for reflective activities that were initiated by mentors through the provision of templates of reflection, questionnaire, and reflective journal; and independent reflective practice for reflective activities that were initiated by novice teachers themselves through immersing into critical thinking and analysing about their practice. While it is important for mentors to assist novice teachers to develop their reflective skills through supported reflective activities, mentors should encourage novice teachers to continue their reflective practice even when they have completed the mentoring programme by engaging in independent reflective practice autonomously. Hence, mentors should raise novice teachers' awareness about the value of reflective practice in order for them to continue engaging in reflective practice by transforming the supported reflective activities that they learn during mentoring programme into independent reflective practice that they engage in after the programme.

As a whole, the case studies provide evidence for the participating ESL novice teachers in having valuable opportunities to share their stories on the changes that they experienced particularly in their professional knowledge construction, professional practice establishment, and professional identity formation as a result from their participation in the *Native Speaker Programme*. These reflective stories are potentially powerful in allowing the participants to develop a deeper understanding about their professional development as ESL teachers. According to Johnson and Golombek (2002), by sharing their stories with others, teachers are able to reflect on their practice as their stories enlighten themselves about how their thoughts, perceptions, interpretations, and experience influence their practice. Farrell (2013) asserted that

> These self-reflective stories can provide a rich source of teacher-generated information that allows them to reflect on how they got where they are today, how they conduct practice, the thinking and problem-solving they employ during their practice, and their underlying assumptions, values and beliefs that have ruled their past and current practices
>
> (Farrell, 2013, p. 80)

Through the present study, the participating novice teachers were able to recognize their strengths and weaknesses as ESL teachers. Hence, this ability to reflect could motivate them to improve themselves as ESL teachers in order to better serve the needs of their young ESL learners.

Novice teacher identity formation

An understanding of transforming of identities during the early years of teachers' career is important. Novice teachers undergo shifts in identities from pre-service teachers to professionals as they move from teacher education programme and assume teaching positions. Kanno and Stuart (2011) maintain that transition of identities is not smooth but full of challenges and it is through sustained experience that they come to develop their identities as language teacher. Beijaard, Meijer, and Verloop (2004) elaborate further by stating that a teacher's identity is constantly developing and involves two strongly interwoven sides: the teacher's own ideas accumulated on the basis of personal experience, and the ideas or expectations imposed upon the teacher by the social context.

The current study provides evidence of how the *Native Speaker Programme* could enhance non-native ESL teachers' self-confidence in embracing their 'non-nativeness' by demystifying the native speaker notion. The case studies discussed in Chapter 8 showed that at the beginning of the programme, Hafiz felt inferior about his status as a non-native speaker as he did not have the native-like accent. He believed that the native speaker makes better English language teacher. However, his participation in the *Native Speaker Programme* allowed him to realize the limitation of English native speaker teacher when he noticed his mentors' lack of understanding about the ESL pupils hindered him from suggesting suitable activities for the pupils. Hafiz's realization of his strengths particularly in having a good understanding about his ESL pupils motivates him to embrace his identity as a non-native ESL teacher. Thus, the present study extends the existing research (Golombek & Jordan, 2005; Pavlenko, 2003) that argued teacher education programme has a strong capacity in demystifying the notion of the native speaker.

Furthermore, the present study demonstrated that the *Native Speaker Programme* motivated novice ESL teachers to embrace their identity as non-native teachers by developing a sense of ownership of the English language among themselves. This is evident in Nadya's case as her mentor helped her to realize that English does not exclusively belong to the English native speakers. She also believed that having good command of English language is not necessarily associated with one's nativeness. According to Nadya, "She (her mentor) lets us be ourselves, she lets us be Malaysians, she doesn't push us to have native like accent...and encourages us to use English in our own way". Thus, Nadya's participation in the *Native Speaker Programme* cultivated the notion of ownership of English, hence motivating her to embrace her identity as a non-native English teacher. According to Snow, Kamhi-Stein, and Brinton (2006), ESL teacher development programme must accept non-native teachers' varieties of local English accents and promote a sense of ownership of English language to them so that they can perceive themselves as valuable members of ESL community.

Our study indicated that the *Native Speaker Programme* motivated novice ESL teachers to embrace their identity as non-native teachers by addressing the realities of need in local context. Although the programme aimed at enhancing English language proficiency among the participating teachers, they were not required to achieve native-like accent. All of the participating teachers realized that in their own school contexts, it is not necessary for them to achieve native-like accent. Two of the participants, Farhan and Hafiz, maintained that speaking with native-like accent could make their speech incomprehensible to their young ESL learners, which could be intimidating for them. However, the novice teachers acknowledged the importance of having good command of English as a crucial part of professional identity for all ESL teachers and expressed their intention to improve their language proficiency. Hence, the *Native Speaker Programme* motivated the novice ESL teachers to embrace their non-native teachers' identity by addressing the realities of need in their local context without disregarding their English language competency.

In addition, the present study found that the *Native Speaker Programme* motivated novice ESL teachers to embrace their non-native speaker identity by capitalizing on their strengths as bilingual teachers. This is evident particularly for Suzanna and Nadya as their mentor encouraged and accepted their use of first language in reinforcing students' understanding on classroom instruction. As for Hafiz, the *Native Speaker Programme* encouraged him to capitalize on his strengths as non-native English teacher by providing him the platform for exchange of ideas by interacting with other participating teachers. Although his mentor's lack of understanding about ESL pupils restricted him from suggesting appropriate teaching and learning activities, Hafiz managed to receive support from other participating teachers in the programme. This made Hafiz realize the strengths of non-native ESL teachers, particularly in addressing the need of their learners. The realization motivated Hafiz to embrace his identity a non-native English teacher, as he decided to capitalize on his and other participating teachers' strengths as non-native English teachers in improving his teaching. Chung (2014) argues that non-native English speaker teachers can teach effectively by exploiting their own knowledge on the process of learning English as a second language. Moreover, teachers' awareness about their strengths as a non-native English speaker that they have gained during their second language learning experience serves as a catalyst that leads to their self-empowerment (Chung, 2014).

Moreover, the results of this study found that the *Native Speaker Programme* empowered novice teachers' self-confidence as they began to view themselves as the expert of the field and better teachers and it made them feel appreciated, that they are on the right track, secure, and respected. The programme also promoted positive perception about teaching profession among the novice ESL teachers as they felt satisfied with their career, love teaching, are more optimistic about their roles as ESL teachers, begin to recognize teaching as a rewarding career, and expressed their intention to continue teaching and remain in the profession.

Thus, the case studies indicated that the mentoring programme by the native speakers motivated the novice ESL teachers to embrace their 'non-nativeness' through four ways: by demystifying the native speaker notion, developing a sense of ownership of the English language, addressing the realities of need in local context, and encouraging teachers to capitalize on their strengths as non-native English teachers. Through their participation in this study, the four novice teachers were empowered by their emerging professional identity and gained confidence in their approaches in the classrooms. Kamhi-Stein (2009) asserts that in promoting self-confidence for non-native teacher, it is essential for teacher development programme to address its relevance to non-native teachers' particular value-laden context of practice, since each context has its own specific needs, interests, and expectation pertaining to English language teaching and learning.

One of the implications for future research from the present study is the need for more studies that explore the identity development of non-native English teachers during induction programme in EFL settings in order to enrich the literature corpus on non-native teachers' identity from different contexts. This is because most of the research on such topic are conducted in the Inner Circle countries (Kamhi-Stein, 2009). In light of the struggle experienced by non-native speaker teachers in forming an identity as legitimate ELT professionals due to their non-native linguistic position, mentoring programmes should work on establishing positive self-identifications and promoting their language skills.

Conclusion

Drawing from Kiely and Askham's (2012) construct of *Furnished Imagination* as the conceptual framework for the case studies discussed in this book, the findings provide an insight on the novice ESL teachers' learning through the exploration on the impact of the *Native Speaker Programme* on their professional knowledge construction, practice, and identity formation. This enquiry makes an important contribution to existing literature, as there are so few in this area. It also carries some important implications for teacher educators and policymakers. We argue that if teacher's development programme aims to promote novice teachers' professional knowledge construction, practice and their identity formation, then teacher educators may need to review the design of the programme to address these constructs explicitly through the curriculum of professional courses. This will then facilitate novice teachers to establish sound professional teacher competencies.

Furthermore, in order to develop an effective mentoring programme, teacher educators should identify novice teachers' needs. A tailored induction approach based on the novice teachers' needs would be more beneficial as opposed to the common universal approach. The development and growth of novice teachers provide a vital foundation for the enhancement of professionalism in the teaching profession. Successful mentoring programmes require careful planning and management. Professional development and practices in high-achieving nations reflect many of the principles of effective professional learning, providing sustained and extensive opportunities to develop practice that go well beyond traditional "one-shot" programme approaches.

As Kabilan and Veratharaju (2013) rightly point out, the Malaysian MOE need to assist the schools and teachers with better planning, development, implementation, and assessment of teachers' professional development programme. Improving teacher professional development in a multicultural country like Malaysia requires local solutions, not a one-size-fits-all approach. With a big gap between urban and rural schools, teacher communities in Malaysia have different needs, demographics, and economic circumstances. Teachers need different preparation and support depending on the contexts in which they work. Variations in novice teachers' own prior life experiences and educational background also have implications for the kind of training and support they need. Meeting these needs requires both a variety of preparation pathways and a stronger school and ministry role in co-constructing those pathways with teacher educators.

References

Abell, S. K., Dillon, D. R., Hopkins, C. J., McInerney, W. D., & O'Brien, D. G. (1995). "Somebody to count on": Mentor/intern relationships in a beginning teacher internship program. *Teaching and Teacher Education, 11*(2), 173–188.

Achinstein, B. (2006). New teacher and mentor political literacy: Reading, navigating and transforming induction contexts. *Teachers and Teaching, 12*(2), 123–138.

Ahmad Shah, S. S., Othman, J., & Senom, F. (2017). The pronunciation in ESL lessons: Teachers' beliefs and practices. *Indonesia Journal of Applied Linguistics, 6*(2), 193.

Ali, M.S. (2008). *A case for a case: A qualitative research experience.* Kuala Lumpur, University of Malaya Press.

Avalos, B. (2011). Teacher professional development in teaching and teacher education over ten years. *Teaching and Teacher Education, 27*(1), 10–20.

Barabási, A. L. (2002). Linked: The new science of networks. Cambridge, MA: Perseus.

Bartell, C. (2005). *Cultivating high quality teaching through induction and mentoring.* Thousand Oaks, CA: Corwin Press.

Bartels, N. (2009). Knowledge about language. In A. Burns & J. C. Richards (Eds.), *The Cambridge guide to second language teacher education.* Cambridge: Cambridge University Press.

Bates, A. J., Drits, D., & Ramirez, L. A. (2011). Self-awareness and enactment of supervisory stance: Influences on responsiveness toward student teacher learning. *Teacher Education Quarterly, 38*(3), 69–87.

Beijaard, D., Meijer, P. C., & Verloop, N. (2004). Reconsidering research on teachers' professional identity. *Teaching and Teacher Education, 20,* 107–128.

Bieler, D. (2013). Strengthening new teacher agency through holistic mentoring. *English Journal, 102*(3), 23–32.

Blase, J. (2009). The role of mentors of preservice and inservice teachers. In L. J. Saha & A. G. Dworkin (Eds.), *International handbook of research on teachers and teaching* (pp. 171–181). London: Springer.

Borg, S. (2003). Teacher cognition in language teaching: A review of research on what language teachers think, know, believe, and do. *Language Teaching, 36*(2), 81–109.

Borg, S. (2009). Language teacher cognition. In A. Burns, & J. C. Richards (Eds.), *The Cambridge guide to second language teacher education* (pp. 163–171). Cambridge: Cambridge University Press.

Borg, S. (2010). Contemporary themes in language teacher education. *Foreign Languages in China, 7*(4), 84–89.

Borko, H. (2004). Professional development and teacher learning: Mapping the terrain. *Educational Researcher, 3*(8), 3–15.

Britt, D. C. (1997). Perceptions of beginning teachers: Novice teachers reflect upon their beginning experiences (ERIC Document Reproduction Services No. ED415 218).

Britton, E., Raizen, S., Paine, L., & Huntley, M. A. (2000, March 6–7). *More swimming, less sinking: Perspectives on teacher induction in the U.S. and abroad.* Paper presented to the National Commission on Mathematics and Science Teaching for the 21st Century. Washington, DC: West Ed.

Brock, B., & Grady, M. (2007). *From first-year to first-rate: Principals guiding beginning teachers.* Thousand Oaks, CA: Corwin Press.

Brown, K. (2001). Mentoring and the retention of newly qualified language teachers. *Cambridge Journal of Education, 31*, 69–88.

Burns, A., & Richards, J. C. (Eds.). (2009). *The Cambridge guide to second language teacher education.* Cambridge: Cambridge University Press.

Burton, J. (2009). Reflective practice. In A. Burns & J. C. Richards (Eds.). *The Cambridge guide to second language teacher education.* Cambridge: Cambridge University Press.

Canagarajah, A. S. (1999). Interrogating the "native speaker fallacy": Non-linguistic roots, non-pedagogical results. In G. Braine (Ed.), *Non-native educators in English language teaching* (pp. 77–92). Mahwah, NJ: Lawrence Erlbaum.

Carter, M., & Francis, R. (2001). Mentoring and beginning teachers' workplace learning. *Asia Pacific Journal of Teacher Education, 29*(3), 249–262.

Chapman K. (2009, June 28). Measuring up to new standards. *The Star Online.* Retrieved from http://thestar.com.my

Chen, D., Tigelaar, D., & Verloop, N. (2016). The intercultural identities of nonnative English teachers: An overview of research worldwide. *Asian Education Studies, 1*(2), 9–25.

Chung, K. H. (2014). *Nonnative speaker teachers' professional identities: The effects of teaching experience and linguistic and social contexts* (Unpublished Master Thesis). University of California, Los Angeles.

Clandinin, D. J. (1992). *Classroom practice: Teacher images in action.* London: The Falmer Press.

Clandinin, D. J., & Connelly, F. M. (1987). Teachers' personal knowledge: What counts as 'personal' in the studies of personal. *Journal of Curriculum Studies, 19*(6), 478–500.Clark, C. M., & Peterson, P. L. (1986). Teachers' thought processes. In M. C. Wittrock (Ed.), *Handbook of research on teaching* (3rd ed., pp. 255–296). New York, NY: Macmillan.

Cochran-Smith, M., & Paris, C. L. (1995). Mentor and mentoring: Did Homer have it right? In J. Smyth (Ed.), Critical discourses on teacher development (pp. 181–202). London: Cassell.

Connelly, F. M., & Clandinin, D. J. (1988). *Teachers as curriculum planners: Narratives of experience.* New York, NY: Teachers College Press.

Crandall, J. (2000). Language teacher education. *Annual Review of Applied Linguistics, 20,* 34–55.

Crandall, J., & Christison, M. (2016). An overview of research in English language teacher education and professional development. In J. Crandall & M. Christison (Eds.), *Teacher education and professional development in TESOL: Global perspectives* (pp. 3–34). New York, NY: Routledge.

Creswell, J. W. (2011). *Educational Research: Planning, conducting, and evaluating quantitative and qualitative research* (4th ed.). Boston, MA: Pearson.

Daloz, L. A. (1986). *Effective teaching and mentoring: Realizing the transformational power of adult learning experiences.* San Francisco, CA: Jossey-Bass.

Darling-Hammond, L. (2000). Teacher quality and student achievement: A review of state policy evidence. *Educational Policy Analysis Archives, 8*(1), 7–13.

Darling-Hammond, L. (2006). Constructing 21st-century teacher education. *Journal of Teacher Education, 57*(3), 300–314.

Darling-Hammond, L. (2010). Teacher education and the American future. *Journal of Teacher Education, 61*(1–2), 35–47.

Darling-Hammond, L., Holtzman, D. J., Gatlin, S. J., & Heilig, J. V. (2005). Does teacher preparation matter? Evidence about teacher certification, teach for America, and teacher effectiveness. *Education Policy Analysis Archives,* 13(42), 1–51.

Delaney, Y. A. (2012). Research on mentoring language teachers: Its role in language education. *Foreign Language Annals, 45*(S1), S184–S202.

Deutsch, N. L., & Spencer, R. (2009). Capturing the magic: Assessing the quality of youth mentoring relationships. *New Directions for Youth Development,* 121, 47–70.

DuFour, R. (2004). Professional learning communities: A bandwagon, an idea worth considering, or our best hope for high levels of learning? *Middle School Journal, 39*(1), 4–8.

Dyson, M., Albon, N., & Hutchinson, S. (2007). *Can we improve it? Pre-service teacher education, minimising the negative issues of beginning teachers.* Proceedings of the 2007 Australian Teacher Education Association Conference, University of Wollongong, Australia, 280–290.

Elbaz, F. (1983). *Teacher thinking: A study of practical knowledge.* London: Croom Helm.

Evertson, C., & Smithey, M. (2000). Mentoring effects on protégés' classroom practice: An experimental field study. *Journal of Educational Research, 93,* 294–304.

Ewing, R. A., & Smith, D. L. (2003). Retaining quality beginning teachers in the profession. *English Teaching: Practice and Critique, 2*, 15–32.

Faez, F., & Valeo, A. (2012). TESOL teacher education: Novice teachers' perceptions of their preparedness and efficacy in the classroom. *TESOL Quarterly, 46*(3), 450–471.

Farrell, T. S. C. (2003). Learning to teach English language during the first year: Personal influences and challenges. *Teaching and Teacher Education, 19*, 95–111.

Farrell, T. S. C. (2006). The first year of language teaching: Imposing order. *System, 34*, 211–221.

Farrell, T. S. C. (2008). Here's the book, go teach the class. *RELC Journal, 39*(2), 226–241.

Farrell, T. S. C. (2012). Novice-service language teacher development: Bridging the gap between preservice and in-service education and development. *TESOL Quarterly, 46*(3), 435–449.

Farrell, T. S. C. (2013). Critical incident analysis through narrative reflective practice: A case study. *Iranian Journal of Language Teaching Research, 1* (1), 78–89.

Farrell, T. S. C. (2015). It's not who you are! It's how you teach! Critical competencies associated with effective teaching. *RELC Journal, 46*(1), 79–88.

Farrell, T. S. C. (2016). *From trainee to teacher: Reflective practice for novice teachers*. Bristol, CT: Equinox.

Feiman-Nemser, S. (2001). Helping novices learn to teach: Lessons from an exemplary support teacher. *Journal of Teacher Education, 52*(1), 17–30.

Feiman-Nemser, S. (2003). What new teachers need to learn. *Educational Leadership, 60*(8), 25–29.

Feiman-Nemser, S., & Floden, R. E. (1986). The cultures of teaching. In M. C. Wittrock (Ed.), *Handbook of research on teaching* (pp. 505–526). New York, NY: Macmillan.

Ferrier-Kerr, J. L. (2009). Establishing professional relationships in practicum settings. *Teaching and Teacher Education, 25*(6), 790–797.

Foster, R. (1999). School-based initial teacher training in England and France: Trainee teachers' perspectives compared. *Mentoring and Tutoring: Partnership in Learning, 7*(2), 131–143.

Franke, A., & Dahlgren, L. O. (1996). Conceptions of mentoring: An empirical study of conceptions of mentoring during the school-based teacher education. *Teaching and Teacher Education, 12*(6), 627–641.

Freeman, D. (1996). The "unstudied problem": Research on teacher learning in language teaching. In D. Freeman & J. C. Richards (Eds.), *Teacher learning in language teaching* (pp. 351–378). Cambridge: Cambridge University Press.

Freeman, D. (2001). Second Language Teacher Education. In R. Carter & D. Nunan (Eds.), *The Cambridge Guide to Teaching English to Speakers of Other Languages* (pp. 72–79). Cambridge: CUP.

Freeman, D. (2009). The scope of second language teacher education. In A. Burns & J. C. Richards (Eds.), *The Cambridge guide to second language teacher education* (pp. 11–19). Cambridge: Cambridge University Press.

Freeman, D., & Johnson, K. E. (1998). Reconceptualizing the knowledge-base of language teacher education. *TESOL Quarterly, 32*, 447–464.

Gatbonton, E. (2008). Looking beyond teachers' classroom behaviour: Novice and experienced ESL teachers' pedagogical knowledge. *Language Teaching Research, 12*(2), 161–182.

Goh, P. S. C., & Wong, K. T. (2014). Beginning teachers' conceptions of competency: Implications to educational policy and teacher education in Malaysia. *Educational Research for Policy and Practice, 13*(1): 65–79.

Golombek, P. (1998). A study of language teachers' personal practical knowledge. *TESOL Quarterly, 32*(3), 447–464.

Golombek, P., & Jordan, S. R. (2005). Becoming "lack lambs" not "parrots": A poststructuralist orientation to intelligibility and identity. *TESOL Quarterly, 39*, 513–533.

Gordon, S., & Maxey, S. (2000). *How to help beginning teachers succeed* (2nd ed.). Alexandria, VA: Association for Supervision and Curriculum Development.

Grossman, P. L. (1990). *The making of a teacher: Teacher knowledge and teacher education*. New York, NY: Teachers College Press.

Gu, M., & Benson, P. (2015). The formation of English teacher identities: A cross-cultural investigation. *Language Teaching Research, 3*(19), 2, 187–206.

Halai, A. (2006). Mentoring in-service teachers: Issues of role diversity. *Teaching and Teacher Education, 22*(6), 700–710.

Hall, S. J. (2012). Deconstructing aspects of native speakerism: Reflections from in-service teacher education. *The Journal of Asia TEFL, 9*(3), 107–130.

Hanson-Smith, E. (2006). Communities of practice for pre- and in-service teacher education. In P. Hubbard & M. Levy (Eds.), *Teacher education in CALL* (pp. 300–315). Amsterdam: John Benjamins.

Harrison, J., Dymoke, S., & Pell, T. (2006). Mentoring beginning teachers in secondary schools: An analysis of practice. *Teaching and Teacher Education, 22*, 1055–1067.

Hawley, W., & Valli, L. (1999). The essentials of effective professional development: A new consensus. In L. Darling-Hammond & G. Sykes (Eds.), *Teaching as the learning profession: Handbook of policy and practice* (pp. 127–150). San Francisco, CA: Jossey-Bass.

Hayes, S. B. (2008). *The discursive nature of mentoring: How participation in a mentoring relationship transforms the identities and practices of prospective and practicing teachers* (Doctoral dissertation). University of Florida.

He, Y. (2009). Strength-based mentoring in pre-service teacher education: A literature review. *Mentoring & Tutoring: Partnership in Learning, 17*(3), 263–275.

Hine, A. (2000). *Mirroring effective education through mentoring, metacognition and self-reflection*. Paper presented to Australian Association for Research in Education Conference, Sydney, Australia.

Hobson, A. J. (2009). On being bottom of the pecking order: Beginner teachers' perceptions and experiences of support. *Teacher Development, 13*(4), 299–320.

Hobson, A. J., Ashby, P., Malderez, A., & Tomlinson, P. D. (2009). Mentoring beginning teachers: What we know and what we don't. *Teaching and Teacher Education, 25*, 207–216.

Hudson, P. (2005). Identifying mentoring practices for developing effective primary science teaching. *International Journal of Science Education, 27*(14), 1723–1739.

Hudson, P. (2007). Examining mentors' practices for enhancing preservice teachers' pedagogical development in mathematics and science. *Mentoring & Tutoring: Partnership in Learning, 15*(2), 201–217.

Hudson, P., Savran-Gencer, A., & Uşak, M. (2010). Benchmarking mentoring practices: A case study in Turkey. *Eurasia Journal of Mathematics, Science & Technology Education, 6*(4), 245–252.

Hudson, P., Skamp, K., & Brooks, L. (2005). Development of an instrument: Mentoring for effective primary science teaching. *Science Education, 89*(4), 657–674.

Hudson, S., & Beutel, D. (2007, July). *Teacher induction: What is really happening?* Paper presented at the Australian Teacher Education Association Conference, Wollongong, Australia.

Ibrahim, M. S., Mohamod, Z., & Hj Othman, N. (2008). *Profesional Guru Novis: Model Latihan. Terbitan Fakulti Pendidikan*, Universiti Kebangsaan Malaysia.

Ingersoll, R. M., & Strong, M. (2011). The impact of induction and mentoring programs for beginning teachers: A critical review of the research. *Review of Educational Research, 81*, 201–233.

Izadinia, M. (2015). A closer look at the role of mentor teachers in shaping preservice teachers' professional identity. *Teaching and Teacher Education, 52*, 1–10.

Jacobi, M. (1991). Mentoring and undergraduate academic success: A literature review. *Review of Educational Research, 61*(4), 505–532.

Jamil, H. (2014). Teacher is matter for education quality : A transformation of policy for enhancing the teaching profession in Malaysia. *Journal of International Cooperation in Education, 16*(2), 181–196.

Johnson, K. E. (1996). The role of theory in L2 teacher education. *TESOL Quarterly, 30*, 765–771.

Johnson, K. E. (2006). The sociocultural turn and its challenges for second language teacher education. *TESOL Quarterly, 40*(1), 235–257.

Johnson, K. E. (2009). Trends in second language teacher education. In A. Burns & J. C. Richards (Eds.), *The Cambridge guide to second language teacher education*. Cambridge: Cambridge University Press.

Johnson, S., Berg, J., & Donaldson, M. (2005). *Who stays in teaching and why: A review of the literature on teacher retention*. The project on the next generation of teachers. Harvard Graduate School of Education.

Johnson, W. B., & Huwe, J. M. (2003). *Getting mentored in graduate school.* Washington, DC: American Psychological Association.

Jones, M. (2003) Reconciling personal and professional values and beliefs with the reality of teaching: Finding from an evaluative case study of 10 newly qualified teachers during their year of induction. *Teacher Development, 7*(3), 385–400.

Jonson, K. F. (2002). *The new elementary teacher's handbook: Flourishing in your first year.* Thousand Oaks, CA: Corwin Press.

Kabilan, M. K. (2007). English language teachers reflecting on reflections: A Malaysian experience. *TESOL Quarterly, 41*(4), 681–705.

Kabilan, M. K., Adlina, W. F. W., & Embi, M. A. (2011). Online collaboration of English language teachers for meaningful professional development experiences. *English Teaching: Practice and Critique, 10*(4), 94–115.

Kabilan, M. K., & Veratharaju, K. (2013). Professional development needs of primary school English-language teachers in Malaysia. *Professional Development in Education, 39*(3), 330–351.

Kagan, D. (1992). Professional growth among preservice beginning teachers. *Review of Educational Research, 62*, 129–169.

Kamhi-Stein, L. D. (2009). Teacher preparation and nonnative English-speaking educators. In A. Burns & J. C. Richards (Eds.). (2009). *The Cambridge guide to second language teacher education.* Cambridge: Cambridge University Press.

Kang, Y., & Cheng, X. (2014). Teacher learning in the workplace: A study of the relationship between a novice EFL teacher's classroom practices and cognition development. *Language Teaching Research, 18*, 169–186.

Kanno, Y., & Stuart C. (2011). Learning to become a second language teacher: Identities-in-practice. *Modern Language Journal, 95*(2), 236–252.

Kardos, S. M., & Johnson, S. M. (2007). On their own and presumed expert: New teachers' experience with their colleagues. *Teachers College Record, 109*(9), 2083–2106.

Kiely, R., & Askham, J. (2012). Furnished imagination: The impact of pre-service teacher training on early career work in TESOL. *TESOL Quarterly, 46*(3), 496–518.

Kim, K.-A., & Roth, G. (2011). Novice Teachers and Their Acquisition of Work-Related Information. *Current Issues in Education, 14*(1), 1–28.

Kissau, S. P., & King, E. T. (2014). Peer mentoring second language teachers: A mutually beneficial experience? *Foreign Language Annals, 48*(1), 143–160.

Knapp, M. (2003). Professional development as a policy pathway. *Review of Research in Education, 27*, 109–157.

Kramsch, C. (1997). The privilege of the non-native speaker. *PMLA, 112*, 359–369.

Lave, J., & Wenger, E. (1991). *Situated learning: Legitimate peripheral participation.* Cambridge: Cambridge University Press.

Lave, J., & Wenger, E. (1998). *Communities of Practice: Learning, meaning and identity.* Cambridge: Cambridge University Press.

Le Maistre, C., & Paré, A. (2010). Whatever it takes: How beginning teachers learn to survive. *Teaching and Teacher Education, 26*(3), 559–564.

Lee, J. C., & Feng, S. (2007). Mentoring support and the professional development of beginning teachers: A Chinese perspective. *Mentoring and Tutoring: Partnership in Learning, 15*(3), 243–263.

Leung, C. (2009). Second language teacher professionalism. In A. Burns & J. C. Richards (Eds.), *The Cambridge guide to second language teacher education* (pp. 49–58). Cambridge: Cambridge University Press.

Lindgren, U. (2005). Experiences of beginning teachers in a school-based mentoring program in Sweden. *Educational Studies, 31*(3), 251–263.

Mackey, A., & Gass, S. M. (2005). *Second language research: Methodology and design.* Mahwah, NJ: Lawrence Erlbaum Associates.

Malaysia English Language Teaching Association. (2010) *A report on the forum "to go or not to go native: The role of native speaker teachers and trainers in second and foreign language teaching"* held at the 19th MELTA Conference. Retrieved from www.melta.org.my

Malaysian teacher standards. (2009). Putrajaya: Teacher Education Division.

Malderez, A. (2009). Mentoring. In J. C. Richards & A. Burns (Eds.), *Cambridge guide to second language teacher education* (pp. 259–268). New York, NY: Cambridge University Press.

Malderez, A., & Bodoczky, C. (1999). *Mentor courses: A resource book for trainee and trainers.* Cambridge: Cambridge University Press.

Malderez, A., Hobson, A., Tracey, L., & Kerr, K. (2007). Becoming a student teacher: Core features of the experience. *European Journal of Teacher Education, 30*, 225–248.

Mann, S., & Tang, E. H. H. (2012) The role of mentoring in supporting novice English language teachers in Hong Kong. *TESOL Quarterly, 46*(3), 472–495.

Martin, M., & Rippon, J. (2003). Teacher induction: Personal intelligence and the mentoring relationship. *Journal of In-Service Education, 29*(1), 141–162.

Maynard, T. (2000). Learning to teach or learning to manage mentors? Experiences of school-based teacher training. *Mentoring and Tutoring: Partnership in Learning, 8*(1), 17–30.

Maynard, T., & Furlong, J. (1995). Learning to teach and models of mentoring. In: T. Kelly & A. Mayes (Eds.), *Issues in mentoring.* London: Routledge.

Medgyes, P. (1994). *The non-native teacher.* London: Macmillan.

Meijer, P. C., Verloop, N., & Beijard, D. (1999). Exploring language teachers' practical knowledge about teaching reading comprehension. *Teaching & Teacher Education, 15*, 59–84.

Melnick, S. A., & Meister, D. G. (2008). A comparison of beginning and experienced teachers' concerns. *Educational Research Quarterly, 31*, 39–56.

Mena Marcos, J., & Tillema, H. (2006). Studying studies on teacher reflection and action: An appraisal of research contributions. *Educational Research Review, 1*(2), 112–132.

Menard-Warwick, J. (2008). The cultural and intercultural identities of transnational English teachers: Two case studies from the Americas. *TESOL Quarterly, 42*(4), 617–641.

Merriam, S. B. (1998). *Qualitative research and case study applications in education* (2nd ed.). San Francisco, CA: Jossey-Bass.

Miller, J. (2009). Teacher identity. In A. Burns & J. C. Richards (Eds.), *The Cambridge guide to second language teacher education*. Cambridge: Cambridge University Press.

Ministry of Education. (2010). Novice teachers development program module. Kuala Lumpur: Ministry of Education.

Ministry of Education. (2012). *Malaysian education blueprint 2013–2025*. Malaysia: Ministry of Education.

Ministry of Higher Education & Ministry of Education. (2006). *Professionalism readiness of novice teachers: Suggested training module*. Penerbitan Fakulti Pendidikan: UKM.

Moir, E. (1999). The stages of a teacher's first year. In M. Scherer (Ed.), *A better beginning: Supporting and mentoring new teachers* (pp. 19–23). Alexandria, VA: Association of Supervision and Curriculum Development.

Moir, E. (2009). *Accelerating teacher effectiveness: Lessons learned from two decades of new teacher induction. Phi Delta Kappan, 91*, 14–21.

Moor, H., Halsey, K., Jones, M., Martin, K., Stott, A., Brown, C., & Harland, J. (2005). *Professional development for teachers early in their careers: An evaluation of the early professional development pilot scheme*. Nottingham: Department for Education and Skills.

Moran, A., & Dallat, J. (1995). Promoting reflective practice in initial teacher training. *International Journal of Educational Management*, (9) 5, 20–26.

Moran, P. M. (1996). "I'm not typical": Stories of becoming a Spanish teacher. In D. Freeman & J. C. Richards (Eds.), *Teacher learning in language teaching* (pp. 125–153). Cambridge: Cambridge University Press.

Morel, N. (2014). Setting the stage for collaboration: An essential skill for professional growth. *Delta Kappa Gamma Bulletin, 81*(1), 36–39.

Moussu, L., & Llurda, E. (2008). Non-native English-speaking English language teachers: History and research. *Language Teaching, 41*, 315–348.

Murshidi, R., Konting, M. M., Elias, H., & Fooi, F. S. (2006). Sense of efficacy among beginning teachers in Sarawak. *Teaching Education, 17*, 265–275.

Nespor, J. (1987). The role of beliefs in the practice of teaching. *Journal of Curriculum Studies, 19*(4), 317–328.

Nguyen, T. M. H., & Baldauf Jr., R. B. (2010). Effective peer mentoring for EFL pre-service teachers' instructional practicum practice. *Asian EFL Journal, 12*(3), 40–61.

Odell, S. J., & Ferraro, D. P. (1992). Teacher mentoring and teacher retention. *Journal of Teacher Education, 43*(3), 200–204.

Orland-Barak, L. (2014). Mediation in mentoring: A synthesis of studies in Teaching and Teacher Education. *Teaching and Teacher Education, 44*, 180–188.

Patrick, R. (2013). "Don't rock the boat": Conflicting mentor and pre-service teacher narratives of professional experience. *The Australian Educational Researcher, 40*(2), 207–226.

Pavlenko, A. (2003). "I never knew I was a bilingual": Reimagining teacher identities in TESOL. *Journal of Language, Identity, and Education, 2*, 251–268.

Pennington, M. C., and Richards, J. C. (2016). Teacher identity in language teaching: Integrating personal, contextual, and professional factors. *RELC Journal, 47*(1), 5–23.

Phillips-Jones, L. (2001). *The new mentors & protégés: How to succeed with the new mentoring partnerships.* Grass Valley, CA: Coalition of Counseling Centers.

Pitton, D. E. (2006). *Mentoring novice teachers* (2nd ed.). Thousand Oaks, CA: Corwin Press.

Portner, H. (2003). *Mentoring new teachers* (2nd ed.). Thousand Oaks, CA: Corwin Press.

Putnam, R. T., & Borko, H. (2000). What do new views of knowledge and thinking have to say about research on teacher learning? *Educational Researcher, 29*, 4–16.

Rajuan, M., Beijaard, D., & Verloop, N. (2007). The role of the cooperating teacher: Bridging the gap between the expectations of cooperating teachers and student teachers. *Mentoring & Tutoring, 15*(3), 223–242.

Reid, K. A. (2010). *Examining the knowledge and meanings constructed by novice teachers within a multi-year, standards-based induction and mentoring programme* (Doctoral dissertation). The University of Wisconsin-Madison.

Richards, J. C., & Farrell, T. (2005). *Professional development for language teachers.* Cambridge: Cambridge University Press.

Richards, J. C. (1998). *Beyond training.* Cambridge: Cambridge University Press.

Richards, J. C. (2008). Second language teacher education today. *RELC Journal, 39*, 158–177.

Richards, J. C., & Farrell, T. S. C. (2011). *Practice teaching: A reflective approach.* Cambridge: Cambridge University Press.

Richards, J. C., & Pennington, M. (1998). The first year of teaching. In J. C. Richards (Ed.), *Beyond training: Perspectives on language teacher education* (pp. 173–190). Cambridge: Cambridge University Press.

Richter, D., Kunter, M., Lüdtke, O., Klusmann, U., Anders, Y., & Baumert, J. (2013). How different mentoring approaches affect beginning teachers' development in the first years of practice. *Teaching and Teacher Education, 36*, 166–177.

Rippon, J. H., & Martin, M. (2006). What makes a good induction supporter? *Teaching and Teacher Education, 22*, 84–99.

Roehrig, A. D., Bohn, C. M., Turner, J. E., & Pressley, M. (2008). Mentoring beginning primary teachers for exemplary teaching practices. *Teaching and Teacher Education, 24*, 684–702.

Rogers, C. (2002). Seeing student learning: Teacher change and the role of reflection. *Harvard Educational Review, 72*, 230–253.

Schmidt, M. (2008). Mentoring and being mentored: The story of a novice music teacher's success. *Teaching and Teacher Education, 24*, 635–648.

Senom, F., Zakaria, A. R, & Ahmad Shah, S. S. (2013). Novice teachers' challenges and survival: Where do Malaysian ESL teachers stand? *American Journal of Educational Research, 1*(4), 119–125.

Shulman, L. S. (1987). Knowledge and teaching: Foundations of the new reform. *Harvard Educational Review, 57*(1), 1–22.

Smith, K., & Sela, O. (2005). Action research as a bridge between pre-service teacher education and in-service professional development for students and teacher educators. *European Journal of Teacher Education, 28*, 293–310.

Smith, T. M., & Ingersoll, R. M. (2004). What are the effects of induction and mentoring on beginning teacher turnover? *American Educational Research Journal, 41*(3), 681–714.

Snow, M. A., Kamhi-Stein, L. D., & Brinton, D. (2006). Teacher training for English as a lingua franca. *Annual Review of Applied Linguistics, 26*, 261–281.

Steers van Hamel, D. (2004). *Rethinking mentor roles and relationships: An exploration of discourse communities and beginning teacher identity* (Doctoral dissertation). State University of New York at Binghamton.

Strong, M. (2009). *Effective teacher induction and mentoring: Assessing the evidence.* New York, NY: Teachers College Press.

Ticknor, A. S. (2014). Negotiating professional identities in teacher education: A closer look at the language of one preservice teacher. *The New Educator, 10*(4), 289–305.

Trent, J. (2012). The discursive construction of teacher identity: The experience of NETs in Hong Kong schools. *TESOL Quarterly, 46*(1), 104–126.

Tsang, W. K. (2004). Teachers' personal practical knowledge and interactive decisions. *Language Teaching Research, 8*(2), 163–198.

Udelhofen, S., & Larson K. (2003). *The mentoring year: A step-by-step program for professional development.* Thousand Oaks, CA: Corwin Press.

Ulichny, P. (1996). What's in a methodology? In D. Freeman & J. C. Richards (Eds.), *Teacher learning in language teaching* (pp. 178–196). Cambridge: Cambridge University Press.

Urmston, A., & Pennington, M. C. (2008). The beliefs and practices of novice teachers in Hong Kong: Change and resistance to change in an Asian teaching context. In T. S. C. Farrell (Ed.), *Novice language teachers: Insights and perspectives for the first year* (pp. 89–103). London: Equinox.

Valenčič Zuljan, M., & Vogrinc, J. (2007). A mentor's aid in developing the competences of teacher trainees. *Educational Studies, 33*(4), 373–384.

Vaught, E. C. (2010). *The relationship of professional identity to mentoring for veteran teachers in an urban school district* (Unpublished doctoral dissertation). Arizona State University.

Veenman, S. (1984). Perceived problems of beginning teachers. *Review of Educational Research, 54*, 143–178.

Velez-Rendon, G. (2006). From student to teacher: A successful transition. *Foreign Language Annals, 39*, 320–333.

Vikaraman, S., Mansor, A., & Hamzah, M. (2017). Mentoring and coaching practices for beginner teachers—a need for mentor coaching skills training and principal's support. *Creative Education, 8*(1), 156–169.

Walker, L. (1993). Changing perceptions of efficacy: From student teachers to first-year teachers (Unpublished paper).

Wallace, M. J. (1991). *Training foreign language teachers: A reflective approach.* Cambridge: Cambridge University Press.

Wang, J., & Odell, S. J. (2002). Mentored learning to teach according to standards-based reform: A critical review. *Review of Educational Research, 72*(3), 481–546.

Weasmer, J., & Woods, A. M. (2000). Preventing baptism by fire: Fostering growth in new teachers. *Clearing House, 73*, 171–173.

Wenger, E. (1998). *Communities of practice: Learning, meaning, and identity.* Cambridge: Cambridge University Press.

Whisnant, E., Elliott, K., & Pynchon, S. (2005, July). *A review of literature on beginning teacher induction.* Prepared for the Center for Strengthening the Teaching Profession.

Woods, D. (1996). *Teacher cognition in language teaching: Beliefs, decision-making and classroom practice.* New York, NY: Cambridge University Press.

Wright, T. (2010). Second language teacher education: Review of recent research on practice. *Language Teaching, 43*(3), 259–296.

Xu, H. (2012). Imagined community falling apart: A case study on the transformation of professional identities of novice ESOL teachers in China. *TESOL Quarterly, 46*(3), 568–578.

Xu, H. (2013). From the imagined to the practiced: A case study on novice EFL teachers' professional identity change in China. *Teaching and Teacher Education, 31*(3), 79–86.

Yin, R. K. (2009). *Case study research: Design and methods* (4th ed.). Thousand Oaks, CA: Sage.

Zacharias, N. T. (2010). *The evolving teacher identities of 12 South/East Asian teachers in US graduate programs* (Doctoral thesis). Indiana University of Pennsylvania.

Index

Printed in the United States
by Baker & Taylor Publisher Services